The man on the cover . . . '[Rankop] rode past on his bicycle with a pile of sheets on his head, bath towels over one shoulder and a slopping pitcher of water in his free hand. This was his method of starting out to do up a room in the morning. He could have walked but balancing several things while steering a bicycle over rough ground was much more fun. Housework was enjoyable if he could also ride his bike, and sing while sweeping and making beds. If he hurried he could find time to pick some flowers for the table and arrange a few in his headcloth (Page 103).' — Drawing by Louise Koke.

All drawings in the main text of this book are by Louise G. Koke and almost all photographs are by Robert A. Koke, including the reproductions of paintings by Louise G. Koke. In most cases this is their first publication. The source of other photographs, whenever known, is indicated. Some names have been changed.

Our Hotel in Bali

How two young Americans made a dream come true
~a story of the 1930s

LOUISE G. KOKE

JANUARY BOOKS

Published by January Books, Ltd,
35 Myrtle Crescent,
Wellington 2,
New Zealand.

ISBN 0-9597806-1-0

Correspondence should be sent to
615 Bukit Timah Road,
Singapore 1026.

Design by Chua Ban Har.

Production supervision by
Design 3,
615 Bukit Timah Road,
Singapore 1026.

Printed by
Kim Hup Lee Printing Co Pte Ltd
22 Lim Teck Boo Road
Kim Hup Lee Building
Singapore 1953

The story of the book

The manuscript of Our Hotel in Bali came to light, nearly half a century after it was written, when I was collecting material for a book about Kuta, the resort village in Bali, Indonesia. I knew that a Kuta Beach Hotel had existed in the years before World War II, and went looking for people with memories of those days. The manager of the present Kuta Beach Hotel was helpful, introducing me to a member of the staff whose father had worked for the earlier hotel in the 1930s. That led to my going to Bangli, a small town in the mountains behind Denpasar, the island's capital. There I met the father, Nyoman Tampa, whose name appears often in the pages which follow.

Nyoman Tampa helped me greatly with information about Kuta, and assisted me still more when he mentioned that the hotel's founders were living in the United States. They were Bob and Louise Koke, and he even had their address in Virginia. I wrote, enclosing a copy of a book I had written about Bali by way of reference, Bob wrote back, and soon I was milking them for material on what Kuta was really like in those days.

Better was to come. In one note Bob mentioned that Louise had written a book about their five years in Bali, but because of the war and other complications it had never been published. I asked for a copy. Better come here, Bob replied. And that is how I came to be sitting in their home one spring morning, leafing through the pages which follow. They were enthralling, and when Louise produced a port-folio of superb drawings and photographs of some of her paintings, and Bob produced boxes of photographic negatives from their years in Bali, a decision to publish became inevitable.

When the Kokes arrived in Bali early in 1936, Kuta was untouched. Later Bob Koke wrote in Fortune magazine about their first sight of it: 'One day when we were exploring the island on our hired bicycles, we pedalled through a coconut grove to come out on the most beautiful beach in the world: Clear surf lapping miles of white sand fringed with palms, and no trace of human habitation as far as the eye could see.'

Bob, who had learned photography and other skills while working for Metro-Goldwyn-Mayer in Hollywood, and Louise Garrett, his future wife, a talented artist, were in a mood to stop. They had been travelling in Japan and China, and had fallen in love with Bali. They decided Kuta

was just the place.

'Within three weeks we had leased part of the beach, and in four months we had built on it the Kuta Beach Hotel,' Bob wrote. '. . . We built it native style — little guest houses of bamboo and thatched roofs, bamboo furniture and batik cushions and couch covers . . . The Dutch tourist agents snorted their disapproval and described our hotel as a collection of "dirty native huts". But that description seemed to do us more good than harm . . . Soon we were turning guests away.'

Their life as self-made hoteliers, coping as amateurs with everything from a shortage of money to the differences between Dutch and American diets, lasted for five generally successful years. It ended when Japanese advances south made staying on perilous. The Kokes escaped, but only just, aboard one of the last ships to leave the Indies before the Japanese occupation.

Months later, with Bob off to join the American army, Louise sat down in New York to record their Bali adventure. When she completed her manuscript, it was put away for the duration of the war — and after the war publishers were more interested in stories about the war itself, and about the fate of a world still full of hazards. Where was there room for a tale as gentle, touching and humorous as this one? The manuscript was put away again, and stayed away for decades. Its delayed publication now makes it no less engaging. Our Hotel in Bali is as fresh and entertaining today as it was when it was written in the 1940s.

More, it enlarges our knowledge of the Balinese. Because the Kokes worked so closely and for so long with so many of the islanders, they gained insights just as accurate as those of more scholarly writers such as Miguel Covarrubias, Colin McPhee and Beryl de Zoete. I find it most

⬆ *Bob and Louise Koke in the garden of their home in Virginia, USA, in 1987. — Photograph by David Frenzel.*

6

engaging that Louise Koke almost passingly makes clear details which drive others to prodigious exertions. The Kokes did not profess to study the culture — they were too busy — but they did acquire a surpassing knowledge, presented here with precision and charm.

Meeting the Kokes was useful in other ways, too. First, a persistent tale that 'Captain Cook', whom I took to be the English navigator, had visited Kuta was laid to rest, but only after my daughter had patiently gone through the literature to determine that he never came near the place. 'Captain Cook' was, of course, the Kokes.

Second, I gained insight into conflicting versions of the origins of the first hotel on Kuta beach. One was written by an American woman, Vannine Walker (pen-name Muriel Pearson), who lived in Bali in the 1930s and took a Balinese name, K'tut Tantri. In a book, Revolt in Paradise, she wrote about her first sight of Kuta: 'The beach was magnificent, and without a house or hut. There were a few temples and numerous fishing smacks or praus moored close . . . What a site for a house! . . . The idea entered my head of building an exclusive hotel!'

In her book she says she leased land, then met a Frenchman who said he would provide the money for a hotel if she would provide the land. She agreed and building began. Bungalows were built for K'tut Tantri and the Frenchman on either side of a dirt road, and the hotel followed on her partner's side of the road. The relationship proved difficult, however, and eventually broke down in acrimony first over how the hotel should be run and then over who owned it. Litigation ensued, and later K'tut Tantri turned her house into another hotel, running it in competition with the first one.

The Kokes' account is that they met K'tut Tantri in Denpasar shortly after arriving in Bali and agreed that she would guide them on some of their tours. Later K'tut Tantri, who spoke Balinese, helped the Kokes with arrangements to lease the land in Kuta and to get their hotel built. For a time, Bob Koke says, she also worked with the hotel as a tourist guide. In return for all this a house was built for her nearby. Then disputation developed, the connection came to an end, and K'tut Tantri opened

SINGARAJA

NEGARA

B A L I

BANGLI   AMLAPURA

TABANAN   KLUNGKUNG

GIANYAR

DENPASAR

KUTA

her own hotel.

When Bob and Louise Koke decided that discretion was the better part of valour, and that they must leave Bali rather than fall into Japanese hands, they advised K'tut Tantri to go as well. She declined, and underwent a fearful ordeal as a prisoner. Later she joined the Indonesian side in the war of independence against the Dutch, the revolt she refers to in the title of her book.

It is a measure of the tensions involved that in this book Louise Koke does not mention K'tut Tantri, while in her book K'tut Tantri refers only to her anonymous 'Frenchman'. Oldtimers recall events with amusement — there could have been few secrets in a place as small as Kuta — but they were probably not funny at the time.

Few changes have been made to this text, save to use modern spellings for Indonesian words and placenames. There was a temptation to alter also Louise Koke's use of the word 'boys' to describe the hotel staff, as such usage is now considered insulting. But she did not consider it so — indeed, her writing displays considerable respect and consideration — so the word has been retained. In this and other matters, the reader is asked to allow for changes in attitudes since this book was written.

One change that was not necessary was from the Dutch 'Koeta' to the modern 'Kuta'. The Kokes arrived at this rendering themselves, long before Indonesia's spelling reforms, when they sought to prevent American tourists causing confusion among drivers by asking for 'Ko—ee—ta'. 'Kuta' solved the problem, and the Kuta Beach Hotel it was from the start.

As for its 'dirty native huts' — time has found in favour of Bob and Louise Koke. Professional hoteliers may have derided their separate cottages under the coconut palms, but the style has flourished. All along Kuta beach today, and elsewhere in Bali, and in tourist resorts throughout the tropics, good hotels offer separate, thatched cottages in spacious gardens. For amateurs the Kokes did pretty well. But then, Bali does tend to bring out the best in people.

Hugh Mabbett

Kuala Belait, Brunei.
November, 1986.

8

Contents

We arrive in Bali

Pale green mountains grew out of the mist ahead. Our hearts beat faster as we leaned against the ship's rail, and we smiled at each other. We had arrived at last at the island of Bali in the Dutch East Indies, the island made famous by exotic travellers' tales. This was to be the big adventure of our round the world travels, better even than Japan and China. I would paint and Bob would take photographs for two restful months before we went on to India and Europe.

Well, we were right about the adventure but entirely wrong about the form it would take. Our artistic endeavours were to prove secondary to all others, and our months — and then years — in Bali would not be restful. The part we were to play was the last we could have foreseen.

The mountains were still two-dimensional, that early morning in August, 1936, when a launch came alongside to take all us new arrivals ashore. As we chugged through the glassy calm towards the primitive wooden jetty at Singaraja, on Bali's north coast, the pearl-grey water reflected the triangular sails of small praus. A photograph for Bob. I watched the brown boatmen in flapping pyjama pants, and realised I would have to learn a little Malay or Balinese to persuade such people to pose for me.

The jetty led us into a board and stucco little town where shops

◄ *Women balanced towering piles of pottery on their heads, walking with backs rigid and hips swaying.*

We settled down to enjoying Bali. Our days were happy and exciting as we watched performances and festivals.

14

▲ *There was so much to see. Bob took the picture on the left; the other two are from postcards we bought in Denpasar.*

had no front walls. Wares were jumbled together in cases and on shelves, and families were making themselves at home as if they were in their living rooms — which they probably were. A fat woman on a three-legged stool suckled a baby while reaching for change after making a sale. An old man sitting in a doorway ate rice with his fingers, and when he was finished tossed his banana-leaf plate into the street.

But our curiosity had to wait. The local agent for the Dutch KPM (Koninklijk Paketvaart Maatschappij) shipping company herded us to his nearby office, and then into ancient Buick touring cars for the trip south across the island to Denpasar, the tourist centre.

We had been fairly docile passengers so far on our journey through the islands, going where and when we were told, but a few days before we had been discussing getting away from the tourist trail to see what we could on our own. The regular tours were not only more expensive than we could really afford, but also could show us only what other tourists had seen and written about. All their accounts suggested too much organisation.

Having made such a radical leap, to begin with, as to leave Bob's job in the movies behind and to undertake a journey around the world, we found that our rashness, instead of exhausting the supply, was about to breed more. When we confessed our intentions to the agent, he frowned darkly and muttered about his company taking care of everything, and about us never finding our way around. But now, on our way across Bali, we were committed to the unknown. When we reached Denpasar we would leave our shipmates amid the comforts of the first-class Bali Hotel and strike out on our own.

Every village we passed on that drive over the mountains was a network of walled enclosures — walls of grey-brown dried mud topped with thatch against the rain. Elaborately carved temple gates of bright vermillion brickwork or pale grey stone were dotted every few miles along the route.

◄ *Elaborately carved temple gates . . . were dotted every few miles along the route, and later we would see festival gatherings as well.*

The well-fedness of everything was striking, from the thick foliage to the broad-shouldered men and sturdy women walking with slow dignity along the roadside. All wore sarongs of brown batik or plaid cloth, except for the small children, who were naked. Above the waist, most were uncovered and the young women's breasts, with dark, pointed nipples, stood out in maternal fullness.

Almost everyone was carrying something. Women balanced towering piles of pottery on their heads, walking with backs rigid and hips swaying. Men carried bamboo poles across their shoulders, a heavy sheaf of rice stalks impaled on each end. Two men walked with a fat, black pig suspended from a pole between them, in an openwork basket which fitted so well it could have been woven around him. Huge, fat water buffalo, pale pink or grey, wallowed in roadside streams or lumbered about with tiny children perched like birds on their broad backs.

In Denpasar, the white and antiseptic Bali Hotel was like something out of Miami Beach, a compound of one-storey stucco buildings with red, tile roofs. The manager greeted us with military heel-clicking and offered us accommodation which would include a modern bathroom with running hot water. Inside the hotel not an inch of Balinese decoration was to be seen. We heard, instead of the strains of one of the famous Balinese gamelan orchestras, static from a radio.

The manager listened politely as we asked if there were not some other place to stay in, and finally admitted there was another hotel. 'Is it less expensive than this?' we asked, feeling embarrassed and anxious to remove our shameful shadows from his luxurious threshold.

'Oh, yes,' he answered distantly, as if we would at least not be poisoned. 'You'll be all right there.' We rode down the street a block to the Satria Hotel. It was definitely second class. Here we could look the manager in the eye without cringing.

The bedrooms were in a row, facing the street with an open porch in front, giving maximum ventilation with minimum privacy. We were ushered into a spartan, box-like room half-filled with a bed under a mosquito net. In one corner stood a monstrous black

◄*Part of a temple complex beneath a towering banyan tree — a typical Balinese scene.*

19

wardrobe, suggesting Hollywood equipment for a murder mystery.

Even as we were shown the room, men and women hawkers hung over the porch railing inviting us to buy carvings, handwoven cloth, silver cups, krisses (wavy-bladed daggers) and masks. 'Very cheap . . . three guilders . . . very old . . . two guilders . . . you want?' they said in English.

Tea was served immediately. Everywhere in the Dutch East Indies it was as regular as the setting of the sun, and much more frequent, unless you ordered something stronger. As the manager was away, an agreeable Eurasian substituted for him, offering to help us in any way he could.

The following morning we investigated the streets of Denpasar, with their weather-beaten board shacks housing Chinese grocery shops and restaurants, curio and art shops, Bombay-style textile bazaars with silks and batiks. Finally we came to a huge native market covering about three acres. The hubbub was terrific as excited shoppers pushed past each other laughing and arguing with the merchants.

There were stalls selling batiks, crockery, trinkets, baskets, mats, kitchenware cleverly made from kerosene tins. Huge baskets overflowed with damp salt made from seawater, roots of all kinds, onions and garlic, an abundance of exotic fruit. Walls of small, tubular baskets containing palm sugar and kapok-filled mattresses crowded a narrow passageway.

Suckling pigs with their legs tied squealed madly as they struggled in the arms of women offering them for sale. Two husky girls thrust their fat-bellied victims at me, screaming in rude competition and laughing at my frightened retreat. Soft, grey ducks cowered in huddles in wide-mesh baskets. Fruits and vegetables rose in tiers all around us, and there were solid banks of tobacco and bright, green sireh leaves, for wrapping betel-nut quids. Stairways led up to shirtmakers with their Singer sewing machines, to clothing stalls, and to still more displays of fruit, chickens, eggs, geese. . . .

Bob and I were enthralled by the energy and humour of the place, by the good-natured banter of the women among themselves and even with us, and by the strenuous bargaining with exaggerated disgust, refusal and final laughing agreement. Already we were beginning to like the Balinese.

In the afternoon we rented bicycles from a Japanese street-stall and rode four and a half miles to Sanur, the nearest beach. The KPM agent had said that two Americans living there might be pleased to see us. As I had not ridden a bicycle since I was eight years old, I could not stop or turn without falling in a tangle of wheels. The roadside ditches drew me like a magnet. In a few minutes the insides of my ankles were raw from hitting metal parts which seemed to be in the wrong places. Bob rode patiently at my side, helped me up after each fall, and had the decency not to laugh.

When we reached the sea we found a coral reef exposed by the low tide and extending two hundred yards out. There were no Balinese girls with flowers in their hair sporting in the limpid waves and courted by men built like brown gods. But then, we should have known better than to confuse Bali with descriptions of Tahiti. We learned later that the Balinese are not swimmers, and that when they bathe they remain strictly segregated.

The home of Jack and Katharane Mershon, when we eventually found it, was small, thatched in the native style, with a carved and gilded doorway and modern bamboo furniture on the porch. The Mershons — dancers who had lived in Bali for years — were so hospitable in spite of our dishevelled appearance that soon we were calling each other by our first names.

A boy of nine, poised and intelligent, served us with drinks made from distilled palm wine, lemon, sugar and soda water. Katharane explained that Murda had come to them three years earlier, insisting on sweeping the yard each morning. 'The next thing we knew he was sweeping the house as well. He could do everything except make the beds — he was too small to reach. Soon he was insisting that we adopt him. His parents came with fruit and flowers, and with tears in their eyes, imploring us to take their boy. They were poor and had too many children. We didn't want the responsibility but eventually gave in.'

'Isn't he homesick?' I asked.

'Oh, no,' Katharane said. 'He goes to school, where he is the brightest pupil, and has many friends. His closest friend is a high caste boy who often spends the night here. They always go through the same formalities. Murda lies on the floor, because he has no caste, and gives the other his bed. But after a few minutes

his friend invites him up and in the morning we find them asleep with their little arms and legs all tangled together.'

The Mershons enjoyed Bali, largely because they kept themselves busy. Jack had coaxed a splendid garden from the sandy, often drought-stricken soil and Katharane ran a clinic for people afraid to go to the government hospital in Denpasar. And they both took great interest in Balinese music and dancing. That night they took us to a rehearsal by their favourite music group, or gamelan.

After the musicians had been playing for a few minutes I realised that one of them, playing a xylophone, was a boy who looked no more than six years old. Katharane explained that he was only five, a musical genius. We watched as he raised a mallet in his diminutive hand to signal pauses and changes in rhythm. He was a strange child with a slightly over-large head and lifeless eyes who never smiled, not even after the performance was over and other children teased him.

Two dancers stepped from the crowd, girls about thirteen or fourteen years of age. They wore batik sarongs to their ankles and their torsos were wound with cloths of various colours, leaving arms and necks bare. Their hair, falling straight down, was sprinkled with a cascade of frangipani blossoms. They danced what Katharane told me was a modified legong, a temple dance they were no longer allowed to perform ceremonially as they had reached adolescence. She had helped them evolve a new routine so they could continue dancing, and all their years of training would not be wasted.

The girls swayed and turned in perfect unison, all their gestures stylised and their movements often as sharp and angular as if they were puppets on strings. Their knees were bent, their feet turned out, their toes upturned. They moved quickly and weaved jagged patterns with their arms and hands, a dance more mathematical than sensual.

When their performance ended, Katharane went up to them and put her arms around their shoulders. Without music, she demon-strated how motions should start at the shoulders and flow down to

◀ *This photograph of dancing girls helped me with my painting — I noted details about the colours of their costumes on the back.*

the fingertips. She was not trying to make them less Balinese, but was showing them a fundamental principle of dancing everywhere that they had forgotten during a few weeks' vacation. The girls imitated her, giggling a little, and recaptured the idea immediately.

As we stood to leave, many people came up to shake hands with the Mershons, talking to them in Malay, obviously on the most friendly terms. The scene, in the glare of a modern pressure lamp, was uncanny — here were short, brown figures, bare above the waist, crowding around four tall foreigners, Bob and I even taller than the Mershons. We went home carrying fruit left over from the refreshments we had been served.

The next day we cycled a few more miles to another beach — to that South Seas picture beach we had been hoping to find. It was at Kuta, as we came to spell it, Koeta as the Dutch preferred. The broad, white beach curved away for miles, huge breakers spread-

ing on the clean sand. Behind were endless coconut groves. Bob tore off his clothes and plunged right in. This was what we had been looking for, not the sun-baked streets of Denpasar and its rows of shacks and shops tended by men in shapeless pyjamas.

Jack Mershon had accompanied us. Now he added a final touch by disappearing for a few minutes and coming back with another girl, another legong dancer, but this time not in costume. In a small, coral temple by the beach, a few altars enclosed by a crumbling wall, she posed unaffectedly for photographs, clad only in her sarong and in the flowers in her long, black hair.

That beach was to loom large in our lives, and the sound of its surf loud in our ears, for years to come.

▼ The broad, white beach curved away for miles, with huge breakers spreading on the clean sand — Kuta beach as we found it.

Girls pose for Bob's camera, one serious, the other with the hint of a smile.

We make our decision

We rented a small house near Denpasar, arranged for meals to be delivered twice a day from a Javanese restaurant, and settled down to enjoying Bali. Our days were happy and exciting as we watched performances and festivals, made friends, and spent hours cycling along hidden lanes and ricefield bunds with paints and cameras. But Bob's photography was always a prelude to panic when we got back home.

A servant, Emal, and I would run backwards and forwards between the well and the porch steps where Bob would be developing his pictures. He had a big dishpan with a block of ice in it, and that pan had to be kept filled with water, each bucket-full filtered through several layers of chamois leather. But no sooner had we filled it than Bob would drain it, and call for still more water.

'Keep it up,' he would say, concentrating intensely. 'More water now, quickly. Hurry up. Careful of that chamois or we'll get dirt on the film. I think I have some good ones of clouds reflected in the ricefields.'

'I can't understand how you can even try to develop film in this house without running water,' I would say. 'This ice Emal gets from the factory looks . . .'

'Fetch more water, Emal,' Bob would break in, muttering between his teeth as he stirred the slippery negatives with one hand and rocked the pan with the other. The professional photographers in Denpasar were liable to scratch his negatives and this

was the only alternative, if he was to produce work as good as his training in Hollywood demanded.

In search of Bali's most popular sport, we followed our guide through a maze of twisting alleys to see a cockfight — one of the illegal variety, unlicensed, the government fee which was supposed to discourage gambling unpaid.

In an enclosed yard, among tumbledown shacks, about two hundred men wandered about and a few old women sat on the ground, rubbing their front teeth with small wads of tobacco. A few men squatted and dandled fighting cocks. An intensely interested group had formed about a man tying a four-inch steel spur on a cock's foot.

Suddenly the first match was ready and two contestants faced each other in the centre of the yard. Each man held his rooster loosely balanced on one hand while with the other he ruffled its neck feathers. Gambling began all around us, and the excitement became almost hysterical.

The fight began. The two birds stalked towards each other with necks outstretched and ruffs widespread. One made a feint, then both jumped together in a furious whirl of feathers. They jumped and flapped, each trying to get above the other so he could stab down with his spur. There was blood on the ground. One bird hobbled off. His owner picked him up, put his beak in his mouth and blew, to give the bird some of his own strength. But the wounded bird declined to fight on.

To finish the contest, both were put under a basket, making flight impossible, and the wounded bird was almost instantly dealt a death blow. The fight had lasted three minutes. As payment for running the show, the 'manager' cut a drumstick from the still jerking corpse. By the end of the afternoon he would have a pot full of chicken for his family.

Later we saw cockfights in conjunction with religious festivals, where they represented a blood sacrifice to the gods. They were tightly packed affairs attended by rajas and their courtiers as well as by the invisible gods watching from high altars. Piles of ringgits,

◄ *Terraced ricefields add to the beauty of a naturally beautiful island.*

silver coins worth two and a half guilders, changed hands in tense betting.

The day after we had watched that illegal cockfight, two men arrived at our house with fighting cocks in the dome-shaped baskets in which they spend almost all their lives. Bob had hired them so he could photograph a fight in progress. He had cut slivers of bamboo to the size of the steel spurs and I had painted them with white tempera so they would show up on the film.

In a sunny space behind our cottage, we had an impromptu audience in no time. Over and over the birds were dandled, ruffled, plucked, and released to stalk and jump at each other. Each jump produced a negative, but there was no telling what was on it until it was developed. This went on for several days until Bob had half a dozen beautiful, clear prints of birds in mid-air, wings spread, glistening spurs jabbing.

The aftermath came quickly. 'Look at these postcards. Aren't they your photographs? They look mighty familiar.'

'My God!' Bob exclaimed, a sudden flush darkening his skin. 'My cockfight! Exclusive photographs I hoped to sell to some good magazine back home. Can you beat it? Where did you get them?'

'From Sagami,' said the two young men from the Bali Hotel with whom Bob had become friendly. Sagami was the Japanese photographer who had made enlargements of Bob's cockfighting pictures.

'And now they're just five-cent postcards for tourists,' Bob said, his face white with anger. 'I'll get that so-and-so. How many were there?'

'Oh, stacks,' the young men said. 'We thought you'd be interested.'

'If I notify the police, will you talk to them for me?'

'Be delighted,' they said. 'Any time. We'll be here another two days.'

The police took testimony from the tourists and found dozens

➤ *A photograph of one of our staged cockfights, with a white-painted bamboo spur gleaming like the real thing.*

*Cockfighting is an important part of the Balinese way of life —
and a spectacular one, full of fury and flashing movement.*

of similar postcards on Sagami's shelves. Eventually the government extracted a fine of thirty guilders ($16.50) from Sagami but such a light fine was no lesson at all to him, or to any of the other photographers in Denpasar. They always made extra prints from tourists' best negatives, even if they scratched or wore them out.

One night we went to the Bali Hotel to see a dance, the kebyar. This was cheating as far as our boastful independence was concerned, since the performance was provided each week for tour members. But it was free to the public also, so we reasoned that we might as well go along.

A baby-faced boy of eight was sitting cross-legged on a raised platform, nearly thirty musicians with their instruments forming a hollow square all about him. He was ornately dressed. One end of a magenta cloth heavily overlaid with flower patterns in gold was wrapped around his hips while the other end stretched out to one side, four feet along the ground. His torso was wrapped in a blue and gold bandage, around his neck he wore a magenta and gold collar, on his head he wore a blue and gold cloth, yellow blossoms were tucked over his ears and a gold poppy on a wire hung trembling over his right temple.

As the music started, tinkling and booming, the little dancer wriggled, rubbed his nose and stretched his long train out on the floor. Suddenly he was alert — transformed. His arms went up, his spread fingers trembling. The innocence of his undeveloped features vanished behind a suggestive, seductive smile.

He performed his entire dance while sitting or hopping in a wide circle with his legs still crossed beneath him, holding his train elegantly between two fingers. The action, all from the hips up, varied from angular, bird-like darts to lithe, sweeping motions. His expression changed from easy repose to surprise, joy, ecstasy, fright, terror. At times his head moved from side to side as if mounted on a horizontal slide. His eyes rolled. His baby lips achieved a supremely honeyed expression. We were completely fascinated by music and dancing so foreign to our experience. That night we went to sleep light-headed in anticipation of more to come.

I negotiated to secure that little boy dancer as a model for a painting. Two days later a ragamuffin in dirty shorts appeared at our porch, a basket on his head.

'Now what do you suppose this is?' I asked Bob. 'The adults find they can't sell us anything, so they send their children to break down our resistance.'

'Don't you recognise your dancer?' Bob replied. 'Wait until he's dressed up and you'll remember.'

'Sougrer, Bli,' I said, using a Balinese phrase for 'Greetings, Brother,' but a little mockingly for this was polite language appropriate for conversation between educated or high caste adults.

'Tabek, Nyonya,' he replied in Malay, putting me firmly in my place as a foreigner.

I never ceased marvelling at the poise and self-control of Balinese children. It surely had something to do with the way they were brought up. No one made a fuss over them. A child with talent might be given dancing lessons and if he became proficient might perform in public, yet his efforts were accepted as naturally as if he had merely added a few words to his vocabulary. If he failed it did not matter.

He told me his name was Nyoman, and began taking his gilded costume from the basket. Neighbours gathered to lend a hand in dressing him — dancing children are always dressed by solicitous elders. He had even brought make-up — black eyebrow pencil, white paste for dots on his forehead, red paper for colouring his lips, yellow powder for his face. Quickly he was transformed into my exotic idol from the Bali Hotel, all ready to be placed cross-legged on a pedestal and wound up like a music box.

When I lifted him on the table, he sat like a log, suddenly sullen and self-conscious. This was a new experience, a little frightening, and he was not sure how to take it. But when I asked him to dance — that was like turning an electric switch. He began a complicated routine, and at the word 'Stop' froze with arms extended, eyes popping. I went to work.

When time came for a rest, no amount of gesturing could convey to him the idea that he was free to walk about, and would be asked to return a few minutes later. He assumed my work was over. I acted out the part, and he caught on. When he saw his likeness appearing on the canvas, he became interested and suggested

changes. 'The skin is too dark . . . my nose is smaller . . . my cloth has more gold,' he said.

Realism was all the Balinese could see in our representations although their own painting is highly stylised, decorative and innocent of perspective.

Late in the morning I tried to persuade Nyoman to eat a banana and drink lemonade.

'I have eaten already,' he said.

I soon learned that this was a routine answer, although most Balinese eat only two meals a day and by mid-morning are fatigued by hunger. New models drove me to despair. They would never touch anything but water. They would not eat in my house because I was only a business acquaintance. But when we became friends they gave in, with a little persuasion, and made me feel less of a slave driver.

During another painting session on the porch, I heard Bob mumbling something about a hotel or guesthouse on the beach at Kuta, where he had gone swimming in the rolling surf. He said it was strange that Kuta had never been appreciated. I was working on a portrait, mopping the perspiration from my face, squinting against the glare.

'It's only six miles from here,' he was saying, 'and on the way to the airport. Something ought to be done about it. It could be a big thing, the opportunity of a lifetime. How about our putting some shacks down there, even nice cottages? You know, Balinese style, servants in native dress, not the white coats that choke the waiters in the Bali Hotel. Can't you hear gamelan music at tea-time? Can't you see the guests wandering among the coconut trees? Think of the . . .'

'Yes, yes,' I said, giving my model a rest. 'It's fun to imagine such a place. But you are really fantastic. Where's the money coming from? And how about the KPM and their Bali Hotel? They catch most of the tourists before they get here. They have them sewn up by getting payment in advance. They're Cooks and American Express agents as well, and they probably control all

◄·*There was so much for me to paint, and models like this girl were rarely reluctant to pose.*

37

other travel bureaus as well. No one would ever hear of us.'

'I'm willing to take a chance,' Bob said, 'if you agree.

'All right.' I said, as you would give a baby a bottle to hush him. 'It's a wonderful idea. But don't you think we should consider it carefully? Let's talk about it this evening.'

How could I have known that Bob, the most unbusiness-like person I knew, would turn out to be an inspired opportunist while I, who foresaw many hindrances, did not see the real one — a global war?

After we had talked the idea over, the obstacles seemed to me no less alarming — but the chance of owning a studio by the sea, running out for a swim whenever I wished, and living in beach clothes appealed to me more every time I thought about it. How many people would give anything for such an opportunity, for a life surrounded by gay and friendly people and for endless enter-tainment? Why not be rash, I thought, and try it? Even if it were only a small business it could support us. And if it failed we could still go home.

'You may have something,' I admitted finally. 'But we might lose our shirts. We would have to sink every cent we have left in it. There would be nothing for a second start. What makes you think we even have enough money to start with?'

'I'm sure we have,' Bob replied. 'Balinese construction is very cheap. We'll have to make the cottages very primitive but we'll have lots of atmosphere.'

'Perhaps you can do it,' I said. 'All I want is a studio where I can paint pictures to sell to your tourists. I'll have to leave the building and running to you. Neither of us has the remotest idea of how to run a hotel but perhaps you can find out how it's done.'

Then, as an afterthought, I added, 'I could help with the house-keeping.'

In a short time I was so deeply interested, so submerged in the venture that I regretted my initial hesitation.

We found a cheap taxi for the first trips to the beach to rent some land. It could not be bought, even if we had had the money, as the wise Netherlands law prevents foreigners buying land in Bali. Bob signed a ten-year lease with the owners for enough ground to take care of expansion beyond our hopes. As the beach was uninhabited, he got it for almost nothing.

We get started

To calm down, I went back to painting and took the caste system by storm, offending at least one person's sense of propriety. He was Gusti Oka, our landlord. His intelligent and aristocratic face with pale brown skin and wide-set eyes made him the most handsome Balinese I had seen. I was very pleased when he agreed to pose for me.

'Sit there,' I said, referring to my dictionary and pushing him on to the table I used instead of a model stand. He laughed and tried to escape while I pressed down on his bare shoulders, repeating, 'Sit, sit!' He was amused but also embarrassed because he saw that when I sat on my chair in front of the canvas I would be lower than him.

The Balinese caste system is built on levels. Gusti Oka (his name indicating his medium caste) did not consider himself superior to me, and so felt it would be presumptuous to sit above me. In the same way, Emal, our servant, having no caste, never spoke to us without squatting or stooping over his clasped hands. Every day we went through the same pantomime. Now Gusti had agreed to pose, but I had to manhandle him into position.

One day a healthy-looking young man came to our house. 'I am sick,' he said. 'When I eat I always throw up. Has Nyonya a pill?'

'No, friend, I cannot give you medicine. There are many kinds of pills and I don't know what kind you need. Have you been to the

*A small selection from my portfolio of Balinese faces, handsome
and full of character.*

hospital?'

'I am afraid to go. Besides, I have no money for the doctor. I bought Chinese medicine but it did not help.'

Perhaps he was afraid of the white doctor and the impersonal formalities of the hospital. Perhaps he did not have a few cents for a week's treatment. But probably he dreaded most leaving his family.

After that he came to us many times, asking us to find him a job. Bob would give him a guilder, about fiftyfive US cents, from time to time, which was all he could do to help.

'I receive a gift,' he would say. 'I will give it back one day if Tuan will give me work.'

'Is there no one in your family who is earning money?' I asked one day.

'No one,' he said. 'My father is too old to work and my sister is very sick. She has been lying down for several months. The jukung [medicine man] can't make her well. Would Tuan be angry if I used this money for a priest? He will ask the gods to help her.'

'Of course you may,' Bob replied — and added with sudden understanding, 'Perhaps the pills are not for you. They are for your sister.'

'Yes, Tuan,' the young man said. 'I hope you will forgive me. I'll invite you and Nyonya to the ceremony.'

A few days later we found ourselves guests in the yard of his house, sitting on specially provided chairs while the whole family sat on mats before their altars — the men crosslegged, the women with legs folded beneath their bodies. The altars were draped with bright cloths and set with edibles such as rice cakes and roast ducks. All present were dressed in their best. The women, scrubbed and with their hair shining with coconut oil, wore white.

The priest, also in white with a giant pink hibiscus flower in the front of his headcloth, sat in front of the altars. A grotesquely large brass ring shone on his slender hand. His finger nails were two inches long. He chanted strange words, rang a long-handled brass bell, moved his hands through graceful gestures. From time to

◄ *A religious occasion under way. The baskets contain offerings. Once the gods have accepted their essence, offerings may be taken home again and consumed.*

time he sprinkled flowers or holy water from a glass jar over shallow baskets of flowers, green leaves and brilliantly coloured rice cakes spread on the ground in front of him.

Behind the priest sat a fat, naked little boy, about two years old, who repeatedly poked at him with wriggling toes. His mother tried to control him and everyone snickered at his antics. After the ceremony everyone was well sprinkled with holy water. As people wandered off, dogs rushed in to snarl and fight over food in the baskets.

We asked to see the sick woman. She was pitiably thin, lying on a bamboo mat in a separate pavilion. Her dishevelled head rested on a hard, dirty, kapok pillow. Although she should have been in hospital, we knew we could do nothing about it and were obliged to leave her to priestly ceremonies and random pills from the Chinese shops.

Later we learned that the Balinese accept illness passively. Few efforts are made towards nursing or medical care. They massage the sick person's legs and feet, administer ground herbs internally and externally, and drench fever cases in cold water or wrap them in blankets. Sometimes they all but exhaust a patient by visiting in hoards and shouting at each other. Those who know say they have very few useful remedies. The jukung sells medicines and magic formulas and recommends certain offerings and rituals. If he fails a priest is called in.

Many believe that the people of that part of the world have discovered one truly effective drug — a secret formula for inducing abortion. Perhaps, but in Bali a violent purgative is used which usually works because it nearly tears the system apart. A girl in trouble goes to some old crone who has acquired the secret, spends a few days in seclusion and returns home with no stigma to follow her through life, though her action is known to everyone in the village.

No stigma, but perhaps she is for a time the butt of some very crude jokes. The Balinese have a robust sense of humour, and find even the most private physiological functions very funny. I once saw a comic interlude in which a clown parodied a woman in labour, rolling on the ground and bellowing. Then another performer

◄*Mother and child — a universal theme.*

dragged a rag doll from under his sarong.

'I believe I can get along without a builder,' Bob said one day, out of the blue. With the confidence of youth, he sounded as if he were contemplating building a chicken coop. His remark brought me back to the reality which I had been trying to avoid. I could not understand how we would build a hotel, let alone run it for tourists.

'You've never made anything except model aeroplanes,' I objected. 'Wouldn't you need to know how the houses are put together?'

'I don't think so. It isn't as if we were building with stucco. I've been talking to some Europeans who live here. I asked how the Balinese make their houses, and it seems every man knows the essentials of construction. They help each other. I want to try it anyway, as I think it will cost less.'

And this in spite of the fact that he could speak only a few sentences of Malay, and that he had no knowledge of materials or of handling Balinese labour.

He hoped to make a deal with a chauffeur named Gusti for buying materials and erecting the temporary shacks we would need while overseeing work on permanent buildings. We went to Labah, a village near Denpasar, looking for him, and found he had a small stucco cottage surrounded by bamboo pavilions — a relatively affluent establishment. As well as being a chauffeur for tourists, he owned his own car and was well known as a gamelan musician and composer. He came to meet us, a young man with the face of a satyr.

After some halting small talk we got down to business, and

◄ *A woman draws water from a well — a photograph for Bob — and, above, a resident poses, a painting for me.*

soon arranged that he would build a small shack on the beach at Kuta. When the price was settled, Bob asked how much he would charge to drive us to Kuta each day.

Gusti bargained, hardly heeding our story about not being rich.

It was obvious he considered all white people wealthy, only some argued about prices while others were too lazy. Eventually it was agreed he would be our driver for a while and help get us started.

While all this was going on, naked children and curious young women peeked around the corner of the house, giggling and whispering. I asked who the women were.

'My wives,' he said.

'May I see them?'

Gusti called, and one by one four women came from the house to stand uncomfortably in front of us, clutching at each other and at their untidy children. They seemed like sisters, all well built and good to look at.

'Are they all your wives?' I asked.

'Yes, I have only four,' Gusti said, motioning them out of sight and returning to more important matters.

So it was that straining coolies began arriving in Kuta, pushing and pulling two-wheeled handcarts laden with bamboo — bamboo bent, split and almost unusable. More came with bricks — bricks crumbling and broken. Our property was a waste of ploughed sand amid the coconut trees. A hedge of weeds and cactus lined the top of the beach. Nothing could have looked more unpromising, and only an enterprising Yankee like Bob could have imagined a thriving and romantic tourist resort amid such desolation.

Day by day twentyfive men sat about in the shade, chewing tobacco, smoking and spitting out red betel juice. For every five who sat gossiping, one would move a stick of bamboo to another place or mix a little cement and slap it around a few bricks. Our daily trips to the beach to see what progress had been made drove me to a frenzy while Bob kidded with the men and treated the whole business as a kind of knitting bee.

But gradually he began to realise he was being taken for a sucker. After two weeks he burst out, 'If I don't fire this gang of incompetents and get some real workers, and a Balinese who knows how to keep them busy, we'll not be able to move down here for another two months.' He admitted failure. We needed a builder who knew the magic formula which made men work.

There was a man living in Ubud, about twenty miles away from Denpasar, named Walter Spies who was reputed to know everything about Bali. Perhaps he would help a fellow white man in distress. Two days later we drove to Ubud.

A dark brown, two-storey house clung to the side of a steep ravine. Dense foliage screened it from the road and made a secret

During five years in Bali I painted whenever our hotel's demands permitted. There was never a shortage of subjects, as every Balinese face was a study in itself.

stillness. Below the house an oval swimming pool lay half hidden among the trees, fed by bamboo pipe from a hillside spring. The house was decorated with Balinese paintings and antique carvings. One of Mr Spies' own paintings, a forest scene in great detail with great shafts of light casting long shadows, hung in the living room. There was a grand piano as well — a remarkable thing to find in such a place.

Mr Spies, tall and dignified, about forty years old, received us cordially and we were soon joined by Miss Vicki Baum, her brother and another German. Miss Baum was doing research for her novel, A Tale of Bali. Two handsome young Balinese men served us with whisky and soda.

At the swimming pool later Mr Spies introduced us to another handsome young Balinese, invited him to show us how well he could swim and dive, and watched him with proud solicitude. The servants brought a low table laden with bottles, glasses and ice and set it in the water at the shallow end of the pool. Mr Spies, lying partly immersed, poured the drinks. I sat up to my waist in the cool, mountain water, holding a glass of Holland gin and imagining what exotic parties could take place in that hidden ravine. At night the wooded slope would be mysteriously lit by burning wicks set in hanging coconut shells. Metal threads in the servants' garments would shimmer in the warm glow. The air would be a little heavy with burning incense, and with the odour of coconut oil in freshly washed and anointed hair.

That was an impression to take away*. We also took away the name of a builder, Krinting.

* *Walter Spies' tropical idyll in that valley near Ubud was not to endure. A colonial government campaign against homosexuals saw him sentenced to imprisonment. In the absence of a jail for white men, he was put in a small house in Denpasar with a room to himself, meals from the Bali Hotel and his painting materials. After four months he emerged in good health and spirits. Another four months in jail in Surabaya followed. Hardly had he put this behind him when Germany invaded Holland and Spies, a German, was arrested again. With the Japanese drawing closer, he and other prisoners were put on two ships bound for Ceylon (now Sri Lanka), but the Japanese sank both of them off*

'We need help,' Bob said. 'Will you make buildings for us? We have land in Kuta'

'I will meet you in Kuta,' Krinting said. 'We shall talk about it.' He was middle-aged, sturdy, with an air of competence. At last, someone to lean on.

'Kuta is a long way from here,' I said.

'It is nothing. I shall put my bicycle on the bus to Denpasar.'

So, a few days later, in Kuta — 'Do you permit me to take charge here?'

Krinting had been watching our indolent coolies sitting about and had seen our bedroom shack, half built of split bamboo and broken bricks.

I wanted to hug him, hoping he would fire every man on the spot and start with a clean slate. But no such satisfaction was possible in this part of Asia, where face must be saved at all costs. Krinting gathered the men together and talked to them quietly for fifteen minutes. When he returned he said, 'I have arranged an overall price. Your little house will be ready in a week.'

Later still, after long conversations, much sketching and some vigorous arm waving — 'Well, it's all settled,' Bob said. 'We sign the contract tomorrow. He is going to build us a dining room, kitchen, a studio for you and me, and four guest cottages. We'll pay half in advance and the rest at intervals. When we sign and hand over the money, there'll be no turning back. We'll be broke until our guests begin to arrive.'

The whole job was going to cost $1375. 'It won't be first class,' Bob said, 'But we haven't the money to do better. It'll be all we need. We can go in for carving and gold doors later.'

We had $1000 with us and could get a little more, so we could count on three meals a day no matter what happened. In a week, once we had moved to Kuta, there would be no more house rent to pay and home cooking would cost less than food from a restaurant.

But what about buying furniture and the thousand other things

the Sumatran coast, and Spies was drowned. His house in Ubud is now part of the Tjampuhan Hotel. He is well remembered in Bali for his considerable contributions to painting, dancing and music.

that a hotel would need? It was a gamble, but by now I was entirely won over.

That night I was so chilled that two coats and two steamer rugs gave no warmth. My teeth chattered and I shivered so much the bed shook.

'You have tertiary malaria,' said the Dutch doctor at the government hospital in Denpasar. 'I'll give you an injection of Atabrine.'

An hour later I felt hilariously well and happy, on a jag better than any from alcohol. Knowing no better, I did not rest. That night the fever was far worse. The next morning the doctor gave me a lecture on the treatment of malaria that both Bob and I had occasion to remember and apply several times in the next few years.

While I was ill Bob signed the contract with Krinting and then went to Mr Smit, the Controleur, or senior official, in Denpasar for a building permit. We had heard he did not like foreigners, or even his own countrymen. He was a small fish magnified by a small puddle.

Consider the way he treated le Meyeur de Merpres, an elderly, gentlemanly Belgian artist living in Sanur. Mr Smit visited him one day to check his permit to live in the Dutch East Indies. He found the artist in his front yard. Dressed in a sarong with no shirt, he was painting a Balinese girl who, like him, wore a sarong with no top. Mr Smit examined the permit and left.

A few days later he notified le Meyeur that he objected to a European wearing native dress — and also to a European painting what he termed 'nude women'. Le Meyeur promptly cabled his friend the King of Belgium, who cabled his friend the Queen of Holland, who cabled the Governor-General of the Dutch East Indies, who wrote to the Resident of Bali and Lombok, who instructed Mr Smit to be nice to le Meyeur. Mr Smit retired to the depths of his puddle to await a more vulnerable victim.

On the strength of all this, we were afraid of Mr Smit — quite rightly, it turned out. Bob did not dare tell him that we planned a small hotel, and said only that we wanted a studio for ourselves and cottages for friends. We got our permit, but there was trouble ahead.

We move to Kuta

Our back porch became a storeroom piled high with furnishings. As there was no ready-made furniture on sale in Bali, I ordered bamboo tables, chairs and beds from a workman in Sanur who had been trained by the Mershons. Kapok mattresses, much thicker than usual, came from an old woman I found rolling a giant swizzle-stick between her palms to separate the down from the seeds and husks. The flying fluff had feathered her shrivelled figure to her eyelashes.

'Adoh!' she said with amusement and disapproval when she examined the measuring strings I brought with me. 'How thick you want them! How can I find so much kapok? I have to carry it many kilometres, and it is heavy as rocks before it is cleaned.'

Her village was a crowded clutter of children, pigs, chickens and dogs with no place to make anything, as far as I could see. But as this was apparently no obstacle we discussed prices, and after prolonged sparring settled on $4.50 for each mattress. The furniture averaged about $1.50 for each item.

Two Chinese shops in town sold everything from American canned goods to blankets and children's toys. I bought kitchen utensils, towels, cheap tableware, small kerosene lamps, pitchers and wash basins. Down a side street, Indian shops sold batiks, artificial silk from Japan and cloth from Holland and England. I bought material for sheets and pillowcases, cheap, ready-made mosquito nets and batiks for table covers and napkins.

The old woman brought one mattress at a time on her head, staggering under a load which would have been heavy for a labourer. She was always snowed over with kapok, rubbing her nose to stop the itching tickle and vainly brushing her drab clothes.

'The Raja of Denpasar saw these and ordered one for himself — but twice as thick,' she exclaimed, chuckling, beginning to appreciate us.

Agung Sindu was a delicate, pretty youth of twentytwo who, like many other sons of well-to-do Balinese families, had been to school in Java.

'Agung, do you know why I have asked you to come?' I said in English after a polite conversation about the weather.

'Yes, I heard you wanted a Malay teacher.'

'Exactly. I am stupid, very slow. Do you think you can stand it?'

'I think I can,' he said with a shy smile.

'I'm working hard furnishing our place in Kuta but I'd like to start straight away, even if we couldn't do more than an hour a day.'

The Malay words I had laboured so hard to memorise would not come together. I was embarrassed at my voice making such strange sounds. It did not seem possible that they meant anything. Agung Sindu was a great relief for at least he could speak a little English.

Like many other educated Balinese, he could find no work to utilise his training and polished manners. A few like him were employed in the banks, post offices and government offices, but the rest, though they felt superior to their uneducated and superstitious countrymen, were idle; not quite belonging to the old Bali yet tied to it by family and religion.

Agung Sindu agreed to teach me Malay in return for $6 a month and meals. His room, like those of our servants, was to be a most primitive cubbyhole with a dirt floor, a bamboo cot and a soap box, but living quarters did not bother him as, like all other Balinese, he spent his time outdoors. We would distinguish his room by giving him a mattress and sheet.

Daily lessons were a tussle, like the extraction of teeth. I seemed to be the teacher and he a rather slow pupil. His timidity drove me to the verge of rudeness, wanting him to force the language into me instead of my dragging it out of him.

'Now, Agung, please make a sentence.'

'What shall I say?'

'Oh, anything!'

'Shall I ask you what time it is?'

'Of course. Anything easy.'

'Pukul berapa, Nyonya?'

'But I know that already. Please put a verb in it.'

'I see. You want a verb. But "pukul" is a verb. At least, it can be.'

'Wait a minute. How do you think we should go about this? How am I going to learn?'

'You say to me in English and I say to you in Malay — all right?'

'Then say, "Cook, I want lunch at one o'clock today".'

Agung said the sentence and I wanted to know why he used 'ask for' instead of 'want'.

'Because "ask for" is polite.'

'Then when may I use "want"?'

'Whenever you wish.'

'Even if it isn't polite?'

'Oh yes, it is polite.'

And so on — to distraction. But Agung Sindu was such an amiable young man that I liked him very much. To keep him entertained as the weeks went by, after we moved to the beach, I spent hours telling him, in English, about life in the United States.

He seemed interested in my descriptions of New York skyscrapers, subways and movie stars. Day after day, I felt I had him spellbound with the wonders of civilisation. In fact I spellbound myself with those long and boastful monologues.

Two months later, when Agung left us to become a tourist guide, he confided to a friend, who told me, that he had not understood a thing I had talked about, and so had suffered acutely from fatigue.

After Gusti was fired for selling us split bamboo and broken bricks, we engaged Made Rai and his seven-passenger Buick. The day we moved to Kuta, Made arrived with his sister, his very pregnant wife and another woman named Rasi.

'Made, is your family going to stay with us?' I asked in constern-
ation.

'Yes, they will stay with us,' he said confidently. 'They can help
a little with the work. You will not pay them. Just feed them.'

'But there is no room,' I protested.

'I will make a bed and put it in the back of the garage. It will be
enough for all of us.'

Rasi was a plump young woman who had once helped a little in
a European household but had not progressed beyond Balinese
cooking. There were no experienced servants unemployed — least
of all a cook. If you wanted a servant, you had to take a boy from
the ricefields or a girl from her village and start by teaching how
to make a bed, how to boil vegetables, how to wash clothes and
so on.

Rasi's wide, flat face was pretty in a sensual way. She wore her
baju, a kind of fitted shirt, so that her billowing breasts were kept
within bounds. I could imagine the difficulty a male guest might
have getting through a meal if those seductive obstacles came between him and his plate every time he was served.

All of us, including Agung Sindu, piled into Made Rai's big car
with as much baggage as possible, and called goodbye to Gusti
Oka and his family.

At the beach the workmen were tying the last swatch of coconut
thatch on to the kitchen roof. Agung Sindu settled into his cubicle
in the garage. Rasi took one and Made Rai the last, letting his
womenfolk shift for themselves until he could make a bed for
them. The privy, two hundred feet behind, was for Bob and me.
The Balinese did not use such conveniences as they felt that all
outdoors was given to them for just this purpose, just as God had
given them hands with which to eat. Even those devoted to
European clothes, pens, bicycles and cars had no use for knives,
forks and bathrooms.

While Made Rai made several trips back to Denpasar to fetch
mattresses and furniture, Bob and I unpacked. Made Rai's sister
and Rasi walked to the market in Kuta village to forage for all of

◄ *Some models eventually found posing irksome and it showed
on their faces . . .*

57

us. The pregnant wife sat in the sun. Agung Sindu, of a high caste family, waited for the first chair to arrive, took it, sat on the porch, and called for tea.

I heard Made Rai mumbling, 'He acts like a raja. He sits on a chair. He asks for tea. Wah!'

Democracy was already undermining the caste system.

Dinner was Rasi's idea of European food. It consisted of a peppery soup of unidentifiable vegetables, rice, shrimps cooked in garlic and rank-smelling coconut oil, and hard-boiled eggs in a yellow sauce overwhelmed by half a dozen roots which give Balinese food its characteristic odour. Dessert was a flat cornstarch pudding touched with rigor mortis.

After dinner I asked Agung to help me talk to Made Rai, for language practice. Made was wearing shirt, coat, sarong and sandals — house servants went barefooted but that was a sign of inferiority. He squatted in a corner and smiled benignly. I cast about for a topic and settled on family life. It was interesting, and such other Balinese favourites as business and religion would be too advanced for me.

I asked Made how many wives he had.

'One,' he replied.

'How long have you been married?'

'We are not married yet.'

'But your wife is pregnant. When are you going to marry her?'

'After she has the baby.'

'But you are so kind, Made, why don't you marry her now?'

'Because I have been married twice before. Both women ran away. I lost much money paying for them and the ceremonies. I will not spend money for a wife again until I am sure she will stay with me.'

'I see your reason. But why do you think she will stay with you after she has the baby? She could take it back to her family. Then you would not have a wife again.'

'Oh, no! The child will belong to me. She cannot take it away.'

Made Rai calculated that his first wives had cost him about 105,000 kepengs. A kepeng — a tiny coin with a hole in it, usually strung together with others in hundreds — was then worth a seventh of a cent, counting in guilders, and a guilder was worth fiftyfive US cents. So Made had lost $82.50, a lot of money for him.

'How much do women usually cost?' I asked. 'They are very expensive in north Bali,' he said. 'A good one is about two hundred guilders ($110). But women are cheaper in south Bali. You can buy one for forty guilders, or less if you have a friend in her family. That's why so many men come here from the north to marry.'

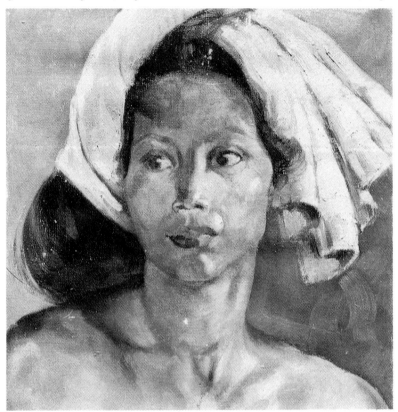

'How about widows and divorced women? Do men want them for wives?'

'Certainly they do. Second-hand ones are very cheap. Sometimes you can get a good one for a ringgit ($1.37).'

We arose to face a breakfast more appalling than the previous night's dinner. The Balinese make coffee by pouring boiling water

▲ . . . *but others were relaxed and serene.*

on the powdered beans, and then drink it thick with grounds. Our beans had been burned instead of roasted, judging by the taste. Fried eggs swam in a lake of butter and the bread, which was singed instead of toasted, had stood in a stack until it was cold and damp from steaming.

I called Rasi and with Agung Sindu explained what was wrong. Rasi looked at me with tears swelling in her eyes. My halting Malay was crude and direct. I did not know the words for instructing her gently. With a sob that shook her full bosom, she removed the dishes and started all over again, while we waited.

After a few days her morale was so broken that she burst into tears at the sight of me. I asked Agung to talk to Rasi, and find out what was wrong.

'Rasi has trouble in the kitchen,' he said on his return, 'because when Made's sister orders her she has to obey, being younger. When she tries to do what you tell her, the sister tells her she is wrong and should do it some other way.'

'Then why don't we get rid of the sister?'

'Perhaps you had better not. You might make Made ashamed, and he would go too. I'll talk to the sister.'

'Fine! Tell her she may have nothing to do with our meals. She may cook for the servants only.'

Matters improved for a while. Rasi could listen to me without weeping and left coconut oil out of the food, but garlic and roots remained as long as she did.

Krinting arrived on his bicycle, all ready to lay out our buildings.

'Have your men started cutting the wood?' Bob asked, not quite believing work would go ahead as promised. Every inch of cutting had to be done by hand, from trees standing in the forest to finished timber with grooved joints.

'The work has begun,' Krinting said with a satisfied smile. 'The men of my village are not lazy like the men of Kuta. Besides, the village headman is my friend. If I have trouble I go to him. When he commands, his people obey. The men of Bongkase are glad to work for me.' Evidently we were dealing with a citizen of influ-

◄ *One for the tourists — why else would a woman hold a coconut thus?*

ence.

Bob sat at the porch table while Krinting insisted on squatting on the floor, a difficult position for drawing plans on the table. He delighted in emphasising his humility by bowing his head with a meek expression when Bob spoke, and by using the most flowery Malay to do the white man honour.

They sketched the positions of the buildings on our lot — 370 ft wide and 234 ft deep — and then paced back and forth, measuring and driving in stakes. They were careful to condemn the smallest possible number of trees. There were to be four cottages in an irregular curve facing the beach, far enough apart to leave room for more later. There would be a large dining room in the centre of the curve with the kitchen behind. Bob and I would have a two-storey studio at one end of the curve, close to the beach.

Two outside bathrooms would have to do for the time being, but we intended to put a private bathroom into each cottage as soon as we could. Later, as we found money to build them, there would also be proper servants' quarters, a permanent garage, a laundry, and so on.

There would be gardens too, if possible without waiting so long. 'We're going to have something that wouldn't shame the House and Garden Magazine,' Bob said. 'We'll have coral paths between the cottages and the dining room, and around each cottage, and the paths will have flowered borders. We'll use what grows around here. The people in Kuta can tell us about that, and I'll write to the botanical gardens at Buitenzorg [now Bogor, near Jakarta] for flowers and shade trees. Father will send seeds from California for a garden.'

The idea of a garden set Made Rai on fire. He borrowed a hoe and spent several days digging up half an acre of sandy soil. He bought several kinds of beans, corn and other seeds and planted them tenderly. He watered them every evening while examining the earth for the first sign of shoots. The corn came up with pale leaves that shot up six inches and stopped. The beans never appeared at all. A few other vegetables struggled to the surface, and immediately withered.

'Never mind,' Bob said. 'We need real earth and fertiliser. I'll get around to it later.'

There would be so many things to get around to later.

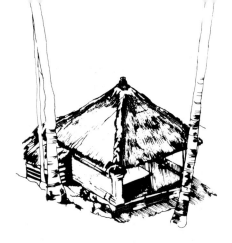

Cremation and construction

Although we foresaw little that lay ahead, it was obvious that providing bed and board would be only half the service that our future guests would expect. Because of Bali's remoteness and its strange language, we would also have to be companions, shoppers, photographers, guides and — because some people were sure to fall ill — nurses. Guiding required that we learn as much as we could about Bali.

Bob bribed boys to cycle from Denpasar with news of dances and festivals, and our servants kept track of anything interesting in the neighbourhood. We were continually adding to what we had learned before moving to the beach, as when we went to Tabanan, a town north-west of Denpasar, for one of Bali's famous cremations. This one was for the wife and daughter of the Raja of Tabanan, who had died some months before.

When we arrived, two huge, white towers taller than the highest coconut palms stood side by side on the town green. Each had eleven tiers — the maximum possible — denoting the high caste of the dead, and each was encrusted with paper and cloth trimmings, artificial flowers, masks and mirrors. On top of one was impaled a large, clumsy aeroplane made of white paper — one of those rare and fleeting foreign touches. Hundreds of colourfully dressed people milled around, and more were arriving every minute.

A high, bamboo ramp leaned against each tower, leading to a platform one-third of the way up. The shrunken corpses, wrapped

in white cloth and trailing many yards more, were carried out through an opening specially knocked in the palace wall — to confuse evil spirits — and up the ramps to their places in the towers. Each tower stood on a latticed bamboo base. Now about fifty men, naked except for loin cloths, stood within and around each base

and, amid great clamour, lifted the two towers to their shoulders and marched off towards the cremation ground.

But it was not a dignified procession, not like one of our funerals. The bearers yelled and grunted, pulled against each other in mock battle, and caused the towers to rock and reel dangerously. A line of women marched ahead, carrying offerings and earthen pots of holy water on their heads. Behind the towers came the raja with his family, some visiting rajas and their families, and other dignitaries. Their women were wrapped in holiday sarongs with bright scarves about their torsos and flowers in their hair.

A royal cremation is not only Bali's most spectacular cultural event but also an event which brings together all elements of that culture. It is colourful, exciting and fascinating. As Bob's photographs on these pages show, it involves hundreds of people — from the artisans who make the tower and coffin to the scores of men who carry the huge structures to the burning ground. A big cremation is something which no visitor to Bali should miss, if he is lucky enough to be there at the right time. During our years in Bali we saw many of them. More photographs on following pages.

Last of all came more men carrying bamboo frames supporting two decorated, carved wooden cows with flaring nostrils and bulging eyes — the coffins in which the corpses would be burned. The bamboo ramps were brought along as well.

At the burning ground (to cut short a long story about one of Bali's most colourful and turbulent occasions) the ramps were placed in position against the towers, the bodies were brought out and down, dragged about, fought over, and eventually, amid much ceremony, placed inside their ornate coffins. Their shrouds were cut open and their faces exposed. Priests with long fingernails intoned prayers and made cabalistic signs. Jars of holy water were poured over the bodies and the jars broken on the ground.

Eventually faggots were placed under and around the cows and set ablaze. Despite their soaking in holy water, they burned briskly. The belly of one cow opened and dumped its contents into the flames. The towers were also set on fire and blazed merrily. Late that day, after we had left, there would be more ceremonies as the ashes of the dead were collected and scattered on running water. And in the days and weeks which followed there would be still more religious occasions, to ensure that the souls of the dead received all earthly help possible to hasten them on their journey to the highest heaven.

Through our years in Bali we collected a variety of experiences at cremations, becoming intimate with their beauty and dramatic ritual, and occasionally experiencing also the appearance and

odour of corpses in all stages of decay. The spectacles varied from the extravagant burning of a raja in effigy to the mass cremation of the remaining bones of fifteen hundred bodies, tied in small

packages and burned in boxes decorated with the wings of dragonflies and butterflies.

Shortly after the Tabanan cremation, and only ten days after Krinting and Bob had staked out our future buildings, a pony cart came galloping in from the road. Krinting followed on his bicycle. His wife was in the cart, along with bundles of rice, clothing and pots.

'What news?' Bob asked. 'When are the workmen coming?'

'Good news,' said Krinting, bowing. 'The men will arrive soon.'

His wife folded a betel quid and handed it to him. He accepted it in silence as there is no word for 'thank you' in Balinese. There is only a phrase meaning 'I ask', which suggests that whatever is given is welcome. The assumption is that when a service is done or something is given it is due or will one day be returned.

Chewing betel and chewing tobacco are more popular than smoking the local cigarettes made of grass, sugar and cloves wrapped in corn husk, and are supplied to guests as we supply cigarettes and drinks. Everywhere, lips are stained red with betel juice and teeth are the colour of mahogany.

No sooner was Krinting happily spitting out vermilion betel juice than a line of barefooted men, women and children came scuffling up the sandy path we had worn from the road. All carried baskets or bundles on their heads. The women wore towels around their heads, but with a loop of hair hanging out at one side. Faded bajus stretched across their muscular shoulders and were fastened between the breasts with safety pins. Below that they were open, flaring out over the hips so that a triangle of bare diaphragm was exposed over the sarong's roll around the waist. Everyone was laughing — except for some gaping at the sea because they had never seen it before.

Although no one seemed to be in charge, everyone went to work and before dark a primitive, lean-to hut had been built against the back of the garage,  made of discarded bamboo and dead coconut fronds. Inside were two long, slat beds, one for men and the other for women. Two women built a fire and boiled rice in an iron pot. Others walked to Kuta village to buy spicy snacks with which to flavour the meal.

The next day Bob and Krinting rigged up a shower for all of us, behind a coconut frond screen beside our old well. They planted a coconut log in the ground so it stood shoulder-high and installed an old, five-gallon earthenware jar on top of it. They had chiselled a hole near the bottom of the jar and cemented in a broken bottle-

neck as a spout. To take a shower you put a cork in the bottle-
neck, filled the jar with a bucket from the well — and then pulled
the cork out.

We took turns bathing there in the late afternoons, after a swim
in the sea. The screen was not really effective, covering only two
sides of a square, but the workers bathed naked with no fear of
being observed. It is the Balinese custom to wash in public places

*⋏ The Balinese bathe frequently, often in special enclosures —
separate for men and women — with permanently running water.*

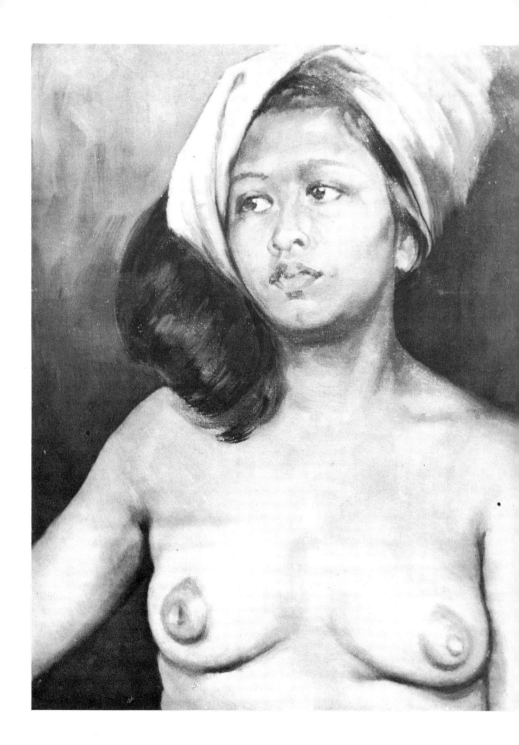

such as rivers and irrigation canals, and while doing so people are considered invisible.

Similarly, a person relieving himself or herself in the open is also invisible, and the workers would just wander off among the coconut trees when they needed to. Privies were not part of their programme. A toilet was built for Bob and me, and for the first few days we were annoyed at finding the seat covered with the prints of large, bare feet. The cause was one of the women workers who was determined to experiment with this new gadget, despite the perilous position. We had to threaten a fine to put a stop to it.

Work began on foundations. With a cross between a hoe and a shovel, the men dug trenches between one and two feet deep, throwing the sand into the centre. With women carrying the bricks, they built walls three to four feet high in the trenches and covered them with a thick layer of cement. When the cement was dry the sand in the centre was soaked and pounded down hard.

'You may not spit on the floor,' I said to the sturdy young woman who was posing for me. 'It is a bad custom.'

She looked at me with dreamy eyes, puzzled, and twitched her mouth, preparing to spit again.

'Out there!' I said, pointing to the ground beyond the porch. 'Not here!' I said, pointing to the blood-red smear of betel juice she had left on the cement floor.

Of course she could not understand Malay, and I had not yet learned Balinese, but my gestures were clear. She heaved herself up with a sigh, arranged the loop of hair which was always escaping from her head towel, aimed a red stream at the sand outside, and returned with a sigh.

Strongly built, with a cafe-au-lait skin, she was one of the workers who did the heavy, unskilled work. I had seen her carrying on her head loads of bricks which two others had had trouble lifting for her. Her muscles were smoothly covered with firm flesh.

I had borrowed her from Krinting for a few days, and she was making more money in a morning posing for me than in three days

◄ This woman posed for me for a few days, but was happy to return to her more active life as a building labourer.

of hard labour. Yet she fidgetted through the last session and left with the first smile since she began. Sitting still and remaining silent must have been taxing indeed. I saw her relief when another fifty-pound load of bricks was lifted on to her head.

One day, with work on the foundations well advanced, Bob felt his face and shook his head as if something rattled inside.

'I think I have a fever,' he said.

His temperature was 102 degrees, and an hour later 104. A tourist who happened by hurried to Denpasar for a doctor.

Hours later, as it seemed, a new sedan car drove up and out stepped a Javanese man in a white suit, a doctor's bag in his hand. The Dutch doctor was not to be found. The moment of strangeness passed. 'Dr Roestam,' he said, standing very straight and shaking my hand — a sure indication of his training in Holland. His matter-of-fact manner gave me confidence.

Bob was throwing his long, thin limbs about the bed, his face flushed and his eyes unfocussed and rolling. Dr Roestam took a blood smear and gave a hypodermic of quinine. The next day he returned to say Bob had malaria tropica, the more serious of the two kinds common in Bali, the other being malaria tertian (my favourite).

Every night for a week, Made and I took turns lying· on chair cushions on the floor beside Bob's bed. During the day, Made rubbed Bob's feet and answered his brass bell — the long-handled kind priests use. I gave him boiled milk and fruit juice, and sponged him with a damp cloth. Dr Roestam came every day, at times injecting morphine to quiet Bob's hysterical reaction to the fever.

The time came to give a glycerine enema. I found it impossible to buy or borrow a bedpan.

'How do you do it?' I asked the doctor.

'You can do what the Balinese do,' he said casually. 'Use a banana leaf.'

Banana leaves are about two feet wide and five or six feet long but are limp and split easily. I tried to visualise the procedure and the probable results.

Bob was humming crazily as I put four chair cushions under his back and a white enamel washbasin close to them, with more cushions under his legs to take the weight off the basin. The treatment was administered without accident.

After a month with us, Rasi relapsed. Every time I corrected her she sniffed and later I would find her in tears. She became slower and more confused.

'Do you think we should put the girl out of her misery?' I asked Bob. 'She isn't learning anything.'

'I certainly do,' Bob said from the couch where he lay, pale and gaunt, recovering from malaria, 'especially after that godawful soup last night. Please don't let anyone use those Balinese onions again. I won't be able to keep them down anymore than I did last time.'

'The matter is serious because we'll soon have tourists to feed,' I said, 'and they'll never stand for the stuff we get now.'

'How about trying a man? The men seem a little hardier.'

So it was that we recruited Nyoman Tampa and Made Rankop from Bangli, twentyfour miles away. Tampa was a lazy, absent-minded adolescent whose whole heart was in the pursuit of girls, because it is only through marriage that a boy becomes a man and a member of the village council. Rankop was about thirty years old and had been a chauffeur in a house where he had seen Dutch cooking. He knew that beds were covered with sheets and that white people had several courses at one meal, with much unnecessary changing of plates and cutlery.

At first, foolishly assuming that anyone could wash clothes, I gave Tampa our laundry to do. Bob's shirts came back shaded from blue through red to green and my dresses were swirls of yellow and purple.

'Tampa, what have you done?' I said severely.

'Nothing, Nyonya,' he said with a broad grin, his big teeth like a mouthful of chalk. 'I washed them as you said, in warm water and much soap.'

But of course he had soaked them with some batik clothes and his own clothes as well.

'They are only a little coloured,' he defended himself as I kept on complaining. 'It is nothing. Another day and I'll do better.'

'Another day,' and every time he did something wrong. He did not like to wash clothes. He wanted to be a cook.

In spite of daily scoldings, Tampa was the soul of good humour and never tired of clowning. I forgave him everything when he wrapped a dish towel around his head, dabbed flour on his face and imitated a girl doing a flirtation dance, or stuck a pillow in his sarong and became a fat tourist getting out of a car. As he grew up he became one of the finest physical specimens we had, and one of the hardest workers. He learned to read and write so he could understand the chits scrawled by tourists and the liquor labels to mix cocktails.

Both men came from poor villages. Tampa had been earning his food and two guilders ($1.10) a month polishing wood carvings. His only experience with white people was as a general utility boy for a Dutchman who took him on a month's camping trip, and occasional housework for a white woman living in his village. Rankop had been all the way to Batavia [now Jakarta] in Java as a chauffeur and was considered a well-travelled citizen. Advanced in his views, he had even allowed his wife to be operated on for a tumour under a general anaesthetic.

But idleness had led Rankop into a serious indiscretion. One night he accosted a Balinese girl — a thing 'not done'. The girl was so frightened that she screamed, her screams were heard, and eventually a police sergeant told Rankop he would have to spend four months in jail. But the jail was full. He would receive a card when there was a vacancy.

Six months later, the card came telling him to report the following week. He was not worried about the disgrace that we might feel at serving such a sentence, for the Balinese do not take such matters very seriously. But he did not want to be deprived of his wife and freedom, and prison food had a bad reputation because no spices were used and rice-millings — pig food —were added to the rice for vitamins.

The woman who occasionally employed Tampa heard of Rankop's case and went to the Controleur to plead for him. He allowed that as a long time had elapsed since the offence was committed, and as four months might seem a little heavy, the sentence could be reduced to four days — if she would employ him.

Thus Tampa and Rankop found themselves working together, and became good friends. With us they both became excellent cooks, and they stayed with us to the end.

Mr Smit strikes

Fortunately for me, I could fight when driven too far. With a dictionary in one hand and a broom in the other, I entered the kitchen. I had been there several times a day with Agung Sindu but in spite of my directions the dirt had become appalling. Perhaps I had not emphasised cleanliness enough for fear of introducing too many new impressions and so getting no meals at all.

I poked about under the built-in counters. In the dark recesses I found mounds of unmentionable rubbish and garbage. Everything was there, from empty boxes and cans to potato parings, eggshells and coffee grounds.

'You must sweep up after every meal, not just once a week,' I explained patiently to Tampa and Rankop, who stood watching with wide eyes. 'You must sweep water over the floor once a day. The garbage pail is for garbage. The rubbish box is for rubbish. When they are full, bury the contents far from the kitchen.'

I understood their confusion as the Balinese have a different disposal system. All scraps are thrown on the ground for the dogs to go over. What is left dries up and is swept away in the morning house-cleaning. They have no boxes or tins to get rid off as food is carried in baskets or wrapped in banana leaves.

A few days later I returned to the kitchen. Shadows had collected in the same dark corners. With a broom I hauled out the same kind of mess I had found before. Blood rushed to my head and savage thoughts stopped at my mouth. Not a word remained from all my lessons and it did not occur to me to swear in English. I simply stood in the middle of the kitchen, hot and strangled. I turned to a furious sweeping, throwing every bit of rubbish all over the yard. I grabbed pails of water and slopped them all over the floor. The embarrassed boys tried to drag the broom from my hands as I sluiced about in the muck. I completed the job and walked out.

From that day on, the kitchen was swept and washed. The garbage and rubbish disappeared. Of course, this did not mean that our ideas of cleanliness prevailed. Few days passed without some instruction in how and what to clean.

Training men to keep the grounds tidy was not easy either. Each of the men who later flatteringly called themselves 'gardeners' had to be put through a week or more of daily grilling before he understood that even such harmless items as pieces of paper, cigarette butts, wads of chewing tobacco, bottle tops and the sheddings from coconut trees were to be cleaned away. They thought us fanatical, if not mentally unbalanced, but excused our eccentricity by allowing that perhaps different people had different customs.

'. . . and you are given ten days in which to liquidate your affairs.'

Bob looked up from the legal paper, his face a greenish-white through the sun tan. 'What is this?' was all he could say.

The Assistant Controleur stood stiffly erect in his starched white suit, his face blank.

'You haven't paid the deposit,' he said stonily.

'But I told the Controleur that the American consul wanted to look into the matter first.'

'Perhaps, but the deposit is overdue and you have no more permission to stay here.'

'Suppose we don't go?' I interrupted. 'What happens then?'

The Assistant Controleur drew in his breath sharply. 'If you and Mr Koke aren't out of the Netherlands Indies in ten days, we shall have to send a police car and put you on a ship. Nothing personal, you understand. Just orders.'

Everything had been going so well. The foundations were almost finished. I had been expecting a few bricks to fall on our heads — but little ones, only now and then. Not this! We, law-abiding citizens, evicted! It was monstrous, impossible! We looked around at those foundations we were so proud of, dazed, too numb to realise fully what was happening.

Mr Smit, the Controleur in Denpasar, was trying to do to us what he had failed to do to le Meyeur. And we did not have the King of the Belgians to help us.

Bob drove to Denpasar immediately, and found the situation fully as serious as we feared. The excuse was a technicality arising from Bob's not paying a deposit the Controleur had demanded six weeks earlier on grounds that he had no income at the moment. The money was to be for our passages home should we become charges on the public. The American consul in Surabaya, in Java, had advised Bob not to pay until he, the consul, investigated and found out if the deposit was according to the law.

Bob telephoned the consul, who told him his letter of inquiry to the Resident of Bali had not been answered. He advised Bob to pay the money at once and promised to wire headquarters in Batavia, asking for an explanation.

When Bob went back to the Controleur, offering to wire California for the money, Mr Smit said, 'I can't accept it now. It is too late. I gave you a month and now it is two weeks overdue.'

Every day we made an agonising trip to Denpasar, hung on to the telephone, hoped the consul would save us before the ten days were up. We dragged ourselves around, our hearts in our throats, pretending to take an interest in the building. The bitter irony of that word 'liquidate'! There was not the least possibility of selling so much as a stick of wood as all of it had been cut to measure. Quantities of bamboo had already been delivered. Matting for walls and tiles for floors were being made to order. We would lose the cost of almost everything except future labour. The government had a reputation for being fair and lenient, so only Mr Smit could be behind this.

On the ninth day, we received a telephone call from the consul saying all was well as the government was willing to accept the deposit. Headquarters in Batavia had not been able to find any reason for the drastic deportation order. 'Be extremely cautious in everything you do, so no future complaints can be brought against you,' the consul advised.

By wiring California for money from the sale of our car, we got

enough to pay the deposit.

A smaller, different kind of crisis followed. We lost our transport. Made Rai left us to take a job with KPM because we could not pay him enough for his car to make it worth his while. Now I had to go to Denpasar in a wobbling, two-wheeled dogcart, a dokka, an aggravating, hour-long trip behind a sweating pony straining under fifty pounds of silver-ornamented harness. Having no icebox, I had to make the trip every other day for meat and vegetables.

An English-speaking boy from our Chinese shop, Peter, helped me with bargaining in the native market. We spent an hour going through the stalls while Peter argued with the women sellers, walking away from each several times before arriving at a reasonable price. We piled our purchases in a large basket on the head of a ten-year-old girl who received two cents for her neck-breaking work.

Peter endeared himself to me with his courtesy and willingness to help, and his shop collected our mail, fetched ice for us from a nearby factory, and ordered beef for us from a butcher who had to sell out before 7 am because of lack of refrigeration. I would also buy glasses or teacups from Japanese shops, or sausages and cheese from a Chinese grocery.

When all was gathered together in the dogcart, one seat would be crushed under a crate of machinery from Java for Bob, baskets of vegetables would overflow on the driver, two tied chickens would be slowly dying of fright on the floor, a suckling pig would lie panting and exhausted, a cake of ice wrapped in newspaper would dribble water down my leg and I would have a box of groceries on my lap. By the time we got to Kuta I would be drenched with perspiration and exhausted.

'Dear Micky,
' . . . Bob and I are building a sort of hotel on a beautiful beach in Bali. We expect to be ready for guests by March first. Perhaps you

◄I painted whenever I could, enjoying Bali's opportunities, as when these young women prepared decorative offerings for a religious ceremony.

could tell your friends or anyone you meet who is headed this way. . . .'

'Who are you writing to?' Bob asked.

'Emily Hahn. She meets a lot of people travelling through Shanghai. I thought she might help us by telling her friends.'

In spite of being a good forager, Rankop was seldom able to buy fish, Kuta's mainstay. Partly because he was also a forager and partly for love of all games, Bob decided to supply the deficiency himself. Elated at the prospect of being able to combine a sport (new to him) with the worthy cause of providing for his household, he approached the subject indirectly by consulting Agung Sindu.

In spite of three gargantuan meals a day, Agung was not getting fat. He was a delicate aristocrat. The rajas we saw at temple celebrations were all husky people of heavy build, but Agung was my idea of what royalty should look like. His almond eyes, long nose with a slight bridge and sensually curved lips were almost feminine.

'I think Agung needs a little outing,' Bob said.

'What's on your mind?' I asked.

'I think he needs a fishing trip.'

'You're not going out in one of those cockleshells?' I asked, a bit worried.

'Why not? The fishermen tell me they've caught baby barracuda near here. I bet the deep-sea fishing is good if you know where to go.'

As he had quite recovered from malaria and was full of excess energy, he organised a fishing party on the spot. Agung accepted his invitation to go along, perhaps just to be relieved of teaching me Malay for one day.

The fishermen of Kuta went out in fleets, guiding their outrigger canoes deftly through the surf. The boats were mere hollowed logs with white beaks projecting from the bows, and with eyes painted to resemble sea monsters. When they got beyond the breakers, the fishermen put up high, triangular, downward-pointing sails and disappeared into the distance.

Fish were not plentiful and a man who came back with four or five pounds of small ones was doing well. Lobster pots, nets thrown into the surf and spearing squid on the reef at night, with flares, helped the village eke out a living.

The morning of our first expedition was busy with tackle to go over and a picnic lunch to prepare. Agung assembled a sun-resistant costume of wide, straw hat, long-sleeved shirt and unbleached muslin sarong. Rankop and Tampa begged to go along but Bob had hired only two boats with their owners, and there was room for only one passenger in each.

Many hands helped run the boats into the water. Bob and Agung stepped in gingerly. The fishermen jumped on to their tiny seats in the stern, and paddled furiously for the invisible line where they could meet a breaker before it had built up too much size and speed. The boats were lifted almost vertically and dropped with a splash on the other side, to slide on safely. In a few minutes sails went up and the boats became smaller and smaller.

When the sun lay a glowing ball on the horizon, Tampa came running to say the boats were returning. There were our fishermen — but how changed! Bob was lobster red with puffy lips. Agung was almost black and tottered feebly up the sand. But Bob was ecstatic as he brought up a forty-pound fish.

'But that's wonderful,' I exclaimed. 'How did you do it?'

'I almost didn't,' he said. 'Agung and I worked all day, holding our poles and pulling in expensive line on expensive reels, getting nothing. All the time the professionals were catching small fish with handlines. We all used the same bait, fish from Benoa. Just as we had given up, I got a strike. The fishermen couldn't believe I could land the thing on such a thin line. Well, I played him for over an hour, and here he is.'

The fishermen stood around, amused at Bob's game of making fishing difficult.

That night Agung was too exhausted to eat dinner. The next day he spent in bed, and the following one in a miserable heap in a corner of the porch. It was Bob's last attempt to build him up.

We still needed a more reliable source of fish for the table.

'What's the matter with this village?' I asked Rankop. 'Why can't you get fish for us?'

'The women selling fish don't come,' he said, absent-mindedly throwing kerosene on charcoal in one of the stoves and lighting it. The flames shot up with a whoosh. I always expected them to set the roof on fire.

'I see women carrying loads of fish to the market in Denpasar,' I persisted. 'Why don't they come here? We are very near and we pay the same prices.'

Rankop fanned the fire. 'They like to go to market,' he said. 'They like to meet their friends and hear the news, that's all.'

He used the word 'ramai', meaning the gaiety of a crowd of people.

'You mean there is no ramai here? You mean that selling to us is work while walking six miles to Denpasar is fun? They would make profit from selling to us. They bargain for half an hour over five cents, so money is important to them.'

'Money is important,' Rankop agreed, wiping the charcoal off his hands with a clean towel. 'But ramai ramai is more important.'

It always was. The excitement of market day found no rival less than a temple celebration or a cremation. The question was, how could we compete?

'I think you had better pay more at first,' I said, 'until they get used to coming to us. Tell them we are going to have many tourists, and will buy much more from them later. The ones who come first will get our business when we are a big hotel.'

Rankop began peeling potatoes, pushing the knife away from him, the reverse of the way we cut.

'Maybe I can get the old Chinese to come here with his dog-cart,' he said. 'He has large shrimps [large as small lobsters]. Usually he takes them to the Bali Hotel. He likes the ride.'

He was referring to an old man we saw often, walking his thin pony along the road, his two crippled legs like dry twigs hanging limply from the front seat. He would touch his ragged cap and blink his one good eye, his shrivelled face always bright with a smile. In his youth he had married a Balinese girl but had mistreated her so outrageously that her family had beaten him with clubs until he was crippled for life.

The people of Kuta did not take us very seriously at first but we knew they would come around gradually as we expanded, and be glad to trade with us.

Our first guests

'Dear Mrs Koke,

'. . . I expect to arrive in Bali with a friend on January 27th. Could you put us up?'

'Look, Bob,' I called in excitement. 'Here is a letter signed "Helen Wright". She heard of us through Emily Hahn and wants to come here with a friend on January 27th. We'll never be ready. What shall we do about it? Our first guests! We must take them.'

'Certainly,' Bob said. 'Write and say we'll be delighted. I'll try to have a cottage ready for them.'

'I suppose you realise they'll have to share our semi-Balinese meals on the porch?'

'What of it? We'll show them a good time. Everything's going to be all right.'

'And you know Krinting's not even started the bathrooms. They'll have to use our privy.'

'They won't mind,' Bob said absently and went back to his book.

Even before Helen Wright arrived, however, we had our first guest. Bill Dunbar, a young American touring the world, heard rumours in Denpasar and came down to investigate. He insisted on staying with us, even though the only place we could put him was on the couch on the crowded porch.

He was good practice for us, though he expected nothing and

never complained. He drank arak and lemon with us every after-noon and put up with Rankop's experiments without a word. I still have a warm feeling for him. He never returned from his visits to Denpasar without a block of ice in his dogcart. For months after he left, occasional travellers who had heard about us from Bill would turn up asking for lodgings. They came in dogcarts, not in taxis . . . and always brought a block of ice.

He helped us celebrate our first Christmas. As it was before we began raising turkeys, I bought a suckling pig from the market and told Rankop to roast it in the Balinese manner. He engaged two men to do the killing and cooking — payment to be a pork dinner afterwards.

One man patiently turned the naked pig, rudely impaled on a bamboo spit held at each end by a forked stick, while the other sat looking vacantly at the smoking fire of coconut leaves. Neigh-bours wandered in to stare at what was happening, as if it were something they had never seen before. We were used to this. Any-thing we did, such as reading a newspaper, eating with knives and forks, swimming in abbreviated bathing suits, seemed of the utmost consequence. Half a day could be spent in close observa-tion without a change of expression.

After an hour and a half, the 'cooks' had reduced the fire to coals for keeping the pig warm until dinner. Horrified at the thought of raw pork, trichinosis and nameless tropical diseases, I told them to proceed with cooking for another hour and a half. They reluctantly added fuel and I left as the smoke was beginning to rise. Ten minutes later I returned to find the fire already sabotaged.

I called Rankop and threatened that if ever pork was cooked for less than three hours, I would 'potong kepala', or cut his head off. It was not an expression to be taken literally. It just meant I was serious. I offered to explain the reason some other time when we had more time.

The dinner did not resemble Christmas in any way. The arak cocktails, the damp heat, the lack of presents because of a lack of money, and the pig meant only Bohemian Europeans having a meal in the tropics.

Before Bill left, Bob had started on furniture.

'Redug, this chair is so crooked I would fall off it,' he said as he sat down and fell grotesquely with legs in the air. The men all doubled up laughing.

'Yes, Tuan, but it is only a little crooked, only kira kira.' 'Kira kira' means 'more or less' and we could think of no way to get that word out of their vocabulary.

Making furniture for Helen Wright and her friend had to be hurried, yet days were being spent on failures. The man in Sanur who could make furniture well was too busy and too expensive. We ordered a few pieces made in a mountain village which claimed to know all about it. The chairs and tables came bristling with nails and already falling to pieces.

Bob decided to take one of the Sanur chairs apart, find out how it was made, and teach others how to do it. Krinting tried to get men to come from Kuta village to learn but none had the courage. Bob tried Legian, a village further along the beach, and persuaded three daring souls to try.

They made a coconut leaf shelter on one of the completed foundations as a workplace. With Bob they took a Sanur chair apart to study the joints and the method of making a slat seat tied with rattan strips. Day after day they worked, holding the bamboo with prehensile toes as they cut and whittled. Gradually a few lopsided chairs appeared. Too many nails showed. The slant of the back was either too much or too little. The seats leaned at drunken angles.

Bob agreed to pay a guilder for each piece, regardless of size or condition, and bought all the first experimental models as encouragement — to be thrown away later. Gradually good chairs and dining tables emerged, and large clothes cupboards, couches, beds and desks with shelves. Even six-sided coffee-tables were invented. Bob began paying more for the larger pieces, up to three and a half guilders.

He stimulated interest by suggesting that other men in Legian could learn the craft and sell to Europeans, Eurasians and Chinese in Denpasar. Later we saw men carrying furniture to town. Legian did good business with the models it learned to make from us.

While Krinting was finishing one cottage in time for the first arrivals and Bob was trying to arrive at usable furniture, I wracked my brains for the cheapest possible method of decorating. We had saved as much money as we could by not buying imported foods or needed clothes. I wore ugly house dresses hurriedly made in China, old sneakers and no makeup.

The solution was inexpensive batik cloth for curtains and couch and cushion covers. I made them on a rented sewing machine trotted down from Kuta village by coolies who suspended it by ropes from a pole. Old Chinese coins much used in Bali made good curtain rings because they had holes in the centre. I made sheets, pillowcases and mosquito nets for the beds.

Our old lady in Denpasar made us three more mattresses of vague dimensions which fitted the beds and porch couch after a fashion. Nothing could be made to exact size, so I could never decide which was better — to have the mattresses made to fit the beds or the beds to fit the mattresses. Both seemed equally unreliable.

To add colour, I painted the wood strips around the woven wall mats vermilion. The result was bright and harmonious.

Now we felt ready for tourists, even if we did not know much about Bali.

The third coat of paint had hardly dried when the afternoon of Helen Wright's expected arrival was upon us. The rain pounded down and water streamed in over the floor. The afternoon turned into evening. We huddled under the porch roof in the dim light of a kerosene lamp, wondering what had happened to her and her friend. They were two hours late. Perhaps they had gone to the Bali Hotel? Perhaps the ship had been delayed? Perhaps their car was lying in a ditch?

A vague light grew out of the darkness, and then a brilliant glare turned the streaks of rain to crystals. Two cars loomed in. Rankop and Tampa ran from the kitchen with Japanese paper umbrellas.

'Is this Mrs Koke?' asked a young woman with a thin, pale face as she ducked under the porch.

'I'm so glad to see you,' I said. 'We were worried about you.'

'We're so relieved to be here, after driving for hours,' she answered weakly. 'My friend couldn't make the trip, I'm sorry to say, but I've brought three people I met on board. They're so anxious to stay with you. I hope you can put them up.'

She introduced two other women and an elderly man, a Mr Harris.

'We'll see what we can do,' I said. 'If you three girls are willing to take the cottage together, we could give Mr Harris one of our rooms and Bob can sleep on the porch. He won't mind a bit. We've only one finished cottage and no dining room yet — I hope you won't mind a little crowding.'

'That's perfect,' said Helen Wright. 'Only please don't let us inconvenience you.'

Inconvenience indeed! I would have slept anywhere myself, just to keep them. It was unthinkable to let any one of them go to the Bali Hotel, because that would have been to admit a measure of defeat at the very start.

But when I took the three women on the long walk through the pouring rain to the privy, with umbrellas and a flashlight, up to our ankles in mud and water, I felt that no beginning could be more unpromising.

Having second thoughts, I told them they would be much more comfortable at the Bali Hotel. 'It isn't too late because one car is still here,' I said. 'I hate to let you go, but . . .'

'I'm staying right here,' said Helen, and the others agreed.

We waited for dinner, trying to keep away from the rain which blew in at odd angles. Tampa appeared under an umbrella with arak, which we drank straight until we felt better.

'Now tell us what happened,' I asked.

'The KPM agent in Singaraja tried to make us go to the Bali Hotel,' Helen began. 'When we told him you were expecting us at Kuta, he seemed very displeased. He argued with us for some time. Then the chauffeurs didn't seem to know where we were going. The two cars separated at one point. They apparently lost their way.'

'That's impossible,' I said. 'They know all the roads like the palms of their hands. They know Kuta just as well as they know Denpasar. And we're just beyond the turn to the airport, which is one of the most important spots on the island.'

'Of course,' Helen said, 'I couldn't understand what the agent said to the chauffeurs, but just before we started he called them back and whispered to them. I thought it was rather strange.'

'No, it wasn't strange at all. He was telling them to make it as

hard as possible for you to get here. He would have offered to pay them for the extra mileage. That agent is burned up at our diverting a few travellers he might have snared for himself.'

Rankop and Tampa came running through the downpour, their bare shoulders glistening with raindrops, to serve us a dinner which can charitably be described as various kinds of stew on rice. It cheered us up.

Then the rain stopped, the floodwater drained away in a few minutes, and at ten o'clock we were all swimming amid sparkling white breakers lit by brilliant moonlight. Everyone was happy. Now nature was on our side.

The money we earned from these guests went into furnishing the second cottage. When more people arrived, we took them in

with low charges and a few apologies. The coconut grove was still an upheaval of construction — but we did have a real bathroom.

'Nyonya, the gamelan of Legian want to play for you,' Rankop said one day. 'They ask if they may come here for dinner. There will be fifty people.'

I thought he meant that we would provide dinner and we talked at cross-purposes until it dawned on me that the musicians and their friends would bring their own food and eat in the garage.

We had listened to the Legian village gamelan, or orchestra, through many evenings and knew some of the musicians by name. It was our business to encourage music and dancing so as to give our guests the opportunity to enjoy them. I told Rankop we would be glad to have the gamelan visit us at any time.

People began strolling in at sundown. Men carried heavy instruments slung on poles, with relatives, friends, swarms of children, and people from other villages as well.

The twentyseven performers and their assistants gathered in our temporary garage. Some had brought baskets of rice, vegetable mixtures soaked in red peppers and roots, and sate — chopped meat skewered on or pressed around sticks, grilled over charcoal and eaten with a spicy sauce.

▲ *Our boys relax with their musical instruments while Bob relaxes with an evening highball.*

With our guests, we watched as they ate dinner with their fingers, in the Balinese manner. I felt ashamed at our rudeness but Rankop said we were not out of order — they did the same to us when they had the chance. Bob gave them several bottles of our best arak.

For the performance, chairs were placed under the trees and the musical instruments arranged in a square formation, with the poles of the heavy, bronze gongs sunk deep in the sand at the back. The music was good but could be improved, as they told us themselves. We suggested they practise some more and said we would hire them for special occasions.

The music was scarcely over when it began to rain. The orchestra manager asked if we would store the instruments overnight under the roof of our new, half-built dining room. Two men would have to sleep with the instruments as a guard, he added, because they cost two thousand guilders and were not yet fully paid for.

'Isn't one enough?' I asked, knowing that one Balinese could sleep as soundly as two.

The manager did not think so, because the beach had many leyaks, or evil spirits. A man alone would be afraid to sleep there. Half an hour of excited argument followed, with everyone reluctant, until four hardy souls agreed to face the long night together.

Tampa went for his kris, his wavy-bladed dagger, and pantomimed attacking a leyak. He lunged and parried, shouting defiance, while everyone chuckled. After subduing the enemy with a quick downward thrust, he handed his kris to the four watchers to keep for the night. But they did not need it.

Danger from evil spirits is greatest nearest the sea — that is, furthest from the mountains above which the gods dwell. Leyaks may appear as blue lights or hideous monsters and the sea is the dwelling place of unknown dangers. This is partly why the Balinese, unlike most island peoples, know little about swimming and are reluctant to fish more than a few miles from shore.

For similar reasons they are reluctant to leave their gods even for a short visit to Java. To add to perils abroad, the Balinese fear that if they die away from home their bodies will not be returned to Bali for the elaborate cremation ceremonies which ensure an afterlife in the heavens.

Balinese building

Krinting was suffering from gallstones, which he blamed on the cold, rain-soaked wind of the west monsoon. By January he was clutching at the region of his kidneys whenever he saw us approaching and murmuring pitifully. Although amused by his play-acting, I was genuinely worried about him.

'What did the doctor say?' I asked.

'The white doctor says I must be cut. He wants me to go to the hospital in Java' — with which he pulled himself together in an expression of agony and gasped for air.

I told him that doctors could put him to sleep and that when he woke up the stones would be gone.

'I've heard the news. They make a man dead, then he lives again. But perhaps I'll remain dead? I would rather die in my village. I'll be better when I leave the beach. The wind enters and makes me sick.'

'But how can the wind get into you when even water cannot get through your skin?'

'Perhaps the Balinese are different. The wind enters our bodies.'

As he resisted all advice, I could do nothing but give him a heavy sweater 'to keep out the wind' which he wore proudly even on the hottest days, sweat glistening at every pore.

The workmen had troubles too. One of them sat on the kitchen foundations with his foot in a pail of hot water and washing soda.

'I told you not to pick that sore,' I said, standing by with a kettle of hot water to add more as the temperature fell. 'You promised to leave the bandage alone. Now look — how swollen your foot is. You must come to me every day to soak it.'

'I only touched it a little,' he said, pouting, 'because it itched.'

Every day several men came to me with holes and lacerations in hands, feet and legs from sharp bamboo splinters. They liked to have me wash their wounds and smear on black antiseptic salve or iodine. Yet no sooner had I bandaged them than they sneaked around the corner and poked their fingers under the edge of the cloth, lifting it to have a look.

Some varied my treatments by removing the bandage altogether and covering their festering wounds with a mixture of mud and ground leaves. The irritants in bamboo and coral sand kept sores running for weeks. When dirty fingers and mud were added, an ulcer might result which would not close for months.

After the first cottage had been completed, the rest went up like mushrooms. Piles of timber lay on low supports to keep it off the ground, each piece marked to show where it would go. With a great straining, conflicting orders and grunted warnings, the pieces were lifted into place and the grooved ends fitted into each other. The joints were secured by drilling holes and hammering in bamboo pegs. Out of Bedlam came the prefabricated skeletons of our houses.

One precaution was always taken. The carpenter had marked each upright with the direction of the tree's growth. The root end must rest on the base because the strength of a tree was an upward thrust. If it were reversed, the house would surely fall down.

But there was a problem with the bamboo. If bamboo for the roof frames had been cut six months before when the sap had receded, it would have been thoroughly dry and uninteresting to boring insects. But as no one kept stocks, Krinting had had to order ours freshly cut at the time the contract was signed. With no time for natural drying, the bamboo had to be cured by soaking in fresh or salt water for two weeks.

The first batch was laid in a concrete trough Krinting built near the sea in our front yard, twenty feet square and three feet deep. When the trough was filled to the brim with bamboo, water was carried from the sea in kerosene tins. Bamboo mats were laid on top to keep out the sun. Underneath, a warm stew festered for a week with a stench more powerful than the ripest corpse at a cremation. We took pains to keep to windward.

When Krinting decided the curing was complete, workers peeled off the mats, releasing an overpowering smell. The heavy poles were dragged out and down to the sea for washing. They were green and brown with mould and decay, but as the men scrubbed them in the waves with pieces of coconut husk they emerged as hard and good as new. Woven bamboo mats for the walls went through the same process.

Later Krinting devised a method which he thought would be easier. He buried bamboo poles three dozen at a time in trenches dug in the sand below the high tide mark. After two or three days the sticks began to rise dancing from their graves, for the waves to hurry them out to sea or along the beach, free for anyone to salvage and take home.

Krinting tore his hair. The waste of it! Was it not bad enough that thieves stole in at night and took poles from the green pyramids stacked against trees to dry. His watchmen were no good. They slept all night though they were paid extra to stay awake. He was losing money. When he finished building the hotel he would be in debt. It did not pay to be honest. Here was he, a sick man, and such troubles made the pain worse. Now he would have to put two watchmen on the beach at night. Adoh!

The watchmen slept peacefully, not even afraid of leyaks, while the bamboo poles continued to drift out to sea. During the day, sudden alarms brought all hands to the rescue. Wild shouting meant the chase was on. Several men stripped off their loin cloths and dashed into the waves with left hands covering their private parts, to drag back the dancing sticks and bury them again.

The treated bamboo was used for roofs, resting on crossbeams at the bottom and the ridge pole at the top, fastened in position with bamboo pegs. Crowded together at the ridge pole and fanning out to the eaves, they looked like the skeleton of an umbrella. The projecting lower ends were sawn off evenly and enclosed in horizontal split bamboo running right around the building.

Thatching was made from a special, tough grass known as lalang. Huge sheaves of it had already arrived, and six men sat all

day folding the grass double over bamboo strips eight feet long and tying it in place. When the roof frame was completed, these eight-foot sections became roofing panels, all ready to be lifted into place. Twenty workers in loin cloths stood on flimsy scaffolding within the roof to tie the panels to the ribs. They used strings of shredded bamboo which had been dyed magenta and which were used when still wet. As they dried they shrank and held the thatching permanently in place.

As with roofing tiles, the lowest panels were lashed into position first — a dejected fringe which looked like a comic decoration. The second panels were only three inches above the first, so the overlap was considerable, and so on all the way to the top. Similar but more complicated methods were used to cover the angles where different planes met. The topmost ridge was sometimes finished with red tiles held in position with bamboo pegs driven into the thick mass of grass underneath. At each cor-

ner an ornamental tile turned the lines of the roof upwards at the ends, like a Chinese pagoda.

As the grass was shaggy and disordered after being laid, it was combed with a rake to put the strands in order. The ragged ends hanging around the eves were trimmed, the workers seeming not to concentrate at all but producing a perfectly horizontal result. After a few rains the roof turned from straw colour to a weathered gray and the thatch seemed glued into place.

After the roof came the floor. Cement an inch thick was poured over the pounded-down sand, and porous brick tiles were laid on the cement. More cement filled the cracks between them. When dry, the surface was smoothed by scraping with a brush made of

↟ Our hotel rooms take shape as workmen pin panels of grass thatching into position. We pioneered the use of Balinese building methods in hotel design.

97

nails hammered close together through a block of wood.

And so on. Door and window frames were pegged into position. Heavy, galvanised wire was stretched between uprights to support the woven bamboo matting panels which would form the walls. Two panels were used for each section, each facing outwards on either side of the wires. Slender bamboo strings barely visible against the basket weave were used to lash the two together. Open spaces between the walls and the tiled floor were filled with still more cement.

At first the buildings, though completed, had a hard and un-cooked appearance. They looked cheap (which they were) and did not blend with the landscape. No wood stain was to be had and paint was too expensive and would not hold up against the weather. The answer, we were told, was used crankcase oil.

Bob bought drums of the tarry stuff and hired four painting women from Denpasar — house painting is not considered manly. Day after day they scrubbed away with stumpy brushes, incredibly slowly, like people working under water. Gradually the cottages became a rich, warm brown, and seemed to grow out of the ground instead of having been awkwardly transplanted.

Anyone intending to live in Bali for two or three years can have a very cheap and attractive house built entirely of bamboo, with coconut frond (not lalang) thatching and cement floors. Glass windows are not possible, but away from the sea wind are not necessary. Mat shutters are made to lock on the inside. Matting can be used for internal partitions. A primitive kitchen, bathroom and servants' quarters can be built outside.

The cheapest bamboo construction when we were there was about $2.50 per square yard of floor area. Our second-grade frame houses cost between $7 and $9 a square yard. The best type, with wooden frame and a thick thatch good for twenty years, was $14 or $15 a square yard.

Potential escapists may be glad to know that, besides being able to build cheaply, they can live well in Bali for $100 a month. Clothes are a minor item. My dresses were made of many kinds of batik and imported English prints by a Chinese seamstress and cost from $3.50 to $6 each. My only footwear was socks and rubber-soled sandals made by a Chinese cobbler for $1.65 a pair.

Grand opening, kitchen-style

'The workmen are ready for the ceremony,' Krinting said. 'You may move into your new kitchen this morning.' As it was the third week in March, he was keeping his promise to complete our buildings within four months.

We had postponed the ceremony while waiting for everyone to return from a three-day celebration in their home villages, as it was necessary for them all to be present. If we moved without the cooperation of the gods, any future calamity would be due to our negligence.

Krinting's wife and some of her friends living nearby had woven small baskets the night before and filled them with flowers and pale leaves from the heart of a coconut tree made into symbolic designs. Early in the morning, the women hung the baskets from all the house corners and burned coconut shell in earthen dishes in each doorway.

We gathered in a circle near the new kitchen. Krinting made a formal speech in Balinese, calling us and our new home to the attention of the gods and asking them to assist in our future prosperity. Tampa passed glasses around and Rankop poured arak into each. After drinking a little, we poured the rest on the ground as an offering.

No Balinese would have felt such a sketchy ceremony sufficient. He would have engaged a priest and made an all-day celebration of it. But being foreigners we could expect consider-

Our hotel gets a name

Weeks passed and we had still not decided on a name, although we needed one for ordering stationery and making road signs. It was my job to design a letterhead and to paint the signs but first we had to know what to call ourselves. Were we a hotel or a furnished bungalows or what? Since we were complete amateurs, we did not feel we had a hotel. The word frightened us. Yet 'furnished bungalows' did not explain that we would take care of meals, laundry, cars, guiding and everything else a tourist needed.

We finally settled on 'Koeta Beach Hotel'. But what about the Dutch spelling? Americans pronounced it 'Ko-ee-ta' and the chauffeurs did not know what they meant. It seemed best to spell it 'Kuta'.

I did a pen and ink sketch of a cottage among the coconut trees with a curving beach in the background. Bob sent it to Java to have stationery printed. A carpenter made us some signboards, and I sketched a design for them as well. Bob took the design to Denpasar to get a government permit.

With this important paper in hand, I bought paints and brushes and began work on the signboards. Rankop, something of an artist and writing a good hand, helped during every minute he could spare from the kitchen. The completed sign, according to the boys, was a great success.

In the centre was a white placard bearing the legend in black, 'Kuta Beach Hotel — R.A. Koke, Manager'. 'Manager' — that sounded like the real thing. Supporting the placard, one on each side, were bright green dragon-gods, five feet high and outlined in black, drawn from the awesome carved guardians of temple gates.

The carpenter bolted the sign to two uprights set in cement and built overhead a small, thatched roof for local colour and to keep the sun and rain off. More signs, on single poles, were planted at strategic places such as the dock at Buleleng, the airfield (only three miles away) and certain crossroads.

Once the signs were up and we had official looking paper for answering inquiries, we felt more sure of ourselves. We forgot we knew little about the hotel business. With mountains before us, we saw only ditches as each day presented more than enough problems for good copers. Daily coping was to become our main concern.

able leniency from the gods.

In a burst of activity, the boys piled the contents of the old kitchen into baskets and rushed them to the new one. Rankop tossed small things into the built-in drawers. A carpenter put up wood strips on the matting walls to hold pots and lids. A second-hand cabinet from Denpasar was fetched from the garage for the dishes. A sack of rice was set in one corner and a covered jar of sugar placed on an empty coffee can in a bowl of water, to keep out the ants.

Bob and Krinting made an oblong frame with shelves, covered it with sackcloth and hung it outside one of the kitchen doors. A can of water hanging above it was punctured so as to drip on the sacking and keep it wet, when the water evaporating kept the whole thing cool. This was the only way to prevent butter melting, and would have to do until we could get a kerosene refrigerator. Left-over meat and vegetables still had to be thrown away each night.

The dining room was also completed, full of yard-square bamboo tables which could be used separately or in a line for a banquet effect. Two couches and two easy chairs with batik covered cushions and a low coffee table stood in each corner. A glassed-in front wall overlooked the beach. We still needed cases for the books which kept trickling in. The bare walls Bob and I eventually were able to decorate with our own photographs and paintings.

A few days later, with the same feeling of adventure that the kitchen and dining room had given us, we moved into our studio — actually mine, for painting, but until we could put up more buildings it was Bob's office as well. Krinting had been worried about the second storey. It overlooked one of the two altars on our land. They were mere piles of stones, but the gods surely came to refresh themselves with the essence of offerings left there. Perhaps it was not proper to sleep in a room higher than any gods who might be visiting? We suggested Krinting get the advice of a priest but eventually he concluded the studio was far enough from the nearest altar to be inoffensive. Besides, since we were foreigners, it might be all right anyway.

The very ·next day, Bob leapt into our studio-office, blond hair on end, waving papers overhead. 'Two telegrams for reservations,' he shouted. 'Not one — two! And wait, that isn't all. There's a letter.

A party of four. We're in business, darling. People are beginning to hear about us.'

We both felt a little professional, with the cottages and dining room finished, with an occasional guest drifting in, and with people booking rooms in advance. But what would happen if we suddenly filled up and had only Tampa and Rankop to do all the work? So far we had taken in guests on the basis that we were not really ready and they must accept us as they found us. But people who booked in advance would want the real thing. We had put off employing more people until we were sure we could pay their wages. We could not delay any longer.

Our guests would arrive within three days of each other, and of course there might be more. We had three weeks in which to prepare. We decided to send Rankop off to Denpasar to find more boys but Tampa found a prospect almost at once.

'There's a man wants to see you,' he called out to me as he rode past on his bicycle with a pile of sheets on his head, bath towels over one shoulder and a slopping pitcher of water in his free hand. This was his method of starting out to do up a room in the morning. He could have walked but balancing several things while steering a bicycle over rough ground was much more fun. Housework was enjoyable if he could also ride his bike, and sing while sweeping and making beds. If he hurried he could find time to pick some flowers for the table and arrange a few in his head-cloth.

By the kitchen I found a tall man with a sweet face and drooping shoulders. His name was Nyongol and he wanted a job as a jongos, or roomboy.

'Have you ever worked as a jongos?'

'No, Nyonya, I don't know anything but I want to learn. I can wash clothes a little.'

Bless his heart! Perhaps he could do better than Tampa, who had damaged everything we had.

'Can you read?'

'I've never been to school.'

Too bad, I thought, since only Tampa could attempt to read the chits that guests would write to order drinks.

'You may work here, Nyongol. When do you want to start?'

'Tomorrow morning, if Nyonya wishes.'

Nothing had been said about wages. He knew that he had to learn first, and that we would give him something in the meantime. Rankop had explained all that.

We paid our boys very little in the beginning because we did not have any money, but they knew their fortunes would rise with ours. They would say, when Tuan and Nyonya eat, we eat, when they die, we die — it was an expression of friendship and sharing. Wages began around five guilders a month and rose to twenty for the best boy. As a guilder was then worth fiftyfive US cents, this must seem inadequate, but the standard of living was on a plane quite different from that in America. We fed the boys, gave them clothes and cared for them when they were sick, and they also got tips. Anyway, we could not pay more, even when the hotel was going full blast, as we had to keep our rates low (from five to ten guilders a day per person, with meals) to compete with other hotels.

Nyongol started by cleaning rooms under Tampa's supervision. When Tampa was supposed to be teaching how to make a bed, I would find him strutting about in a war dance or mincing like a female character in a play, squeaking out a song. The instant he realised I was watching, he would rush to work, and when I laughed he would laugh too, in embarrassment.

Nyongol learned fast. Our clothes and table linen were now washed fairly well and we had an extra hand to help serve meals. Nyongol even picked up some English and practised excruciating phrases on me which sent us both into gales of laughter, such as 'Madam wan tea toast yesterrdahi?' or 'People eat night coming how many you want?' Even Rankop was inspired to try the new language. The first English words he ever spoke, as he showed me a broken tray, were 'What a pity!' — his favourite expression from them on.

The next jongos who came to us was Pougug, who had some experience. Like Nyongol, he was tall, strong and unlettered. A pleasing personality shone from his plain face but white people had spoiled him for his intelligence, and he was oversure of himself. He had to be taken down a flight now and then, and would sit in the kitchen for hours thereafter, holding his head in misery.

Early one morning Pougug demonstrated his knowledge of white men's ways by slapping a Dutch guest resoundingly across

▲ *My painting of a Kuta fisherman, with typical hat and untypical shirt.*

the shoulders and saying cheerily, 'Good morning, Tuan.' If the Dutchman had been paying for his stay, instead of a friend out of a job, he would have packed up and left.

Even boys much less flamboyant than Pougug could run into trouble with our Dutch guests, especially those from Java. I had much to learn.

'I'm not criticising,' a Dutch woman said to me one morning, 'only asking for information. Do you allow your servants to speak to you?'

My heart turned over. It was inconceivable that one of the boys had been rude and yet . . . perhaps one had become confused, and I would have to explain to him after abject apologies to the guest. I asked what had happened.

'Well, this morning, when the boy came to clean the room, he talked to me.'

'What did he say?'

'I don't know. He might have mentioned the weather. Of course, in Java we don't allow a native to address us unless we speak to him first.'

'I've heard of that,' I said, relieved, 'but it's different here.'

After generations of servitude, uneducated Javanese accepted an inferior position. The Balinese, even the unskilled labourers, were still self-respecting and independent. Strangers greeted you on the road as you walked or cycled, asking where you were from or were going to — as a form of greeting, not out of curiosity. If you met your gardener's brother, whom you hardly recognised, he would ask you the news. You observed the amenities by answering 'Good news' and asking some polite question in return. If you snubbed him, you would be both rude and unkind.

'Our boys speak freely to the guests,' I explained. 'They are sure to ask you how long you are going to stay, and perhaps if you are married and how many children you have. If you are pleasant, they will invite you to their village and serve you refreshments as a friend. When we send our boys with guests as guides, they do their best to make people feel they are honoured guests on their island. As they are poor, they respond to tips — but they will do more for you if you are kind. Try it, and you will find they have better manners than many tourists.'

This first lecture became the pattern for many more, except

where the white person was incurable.

One day Nyongol came to me in tears, choking with humiliation, and asked to be given care of a different cottage.

I asked what had happened.

'The guest talked to me so fast I couldn't understand,' he said. 'When I asked him to speak slowly, he said I must be silent. He said I had no manners.' (The phrase for 'no manners' — 'kurang ajar', literally 'no education' or 'no refinement' — is the deepest insult you can fling at a Balinese.)

I went to hear the guest's version.

'I've been running a plantation in Java for twenty years,' he said. 'Don't try to tell me anything about the natives. There isn't one who can talk back to me. I do the talking and they obey.'

'But Nyongol was only asking you to speak more slowly. Most Balinese don't understand Malay as the Javanese do.'

'I don't want to hear anything about it,' he said. 'All he has to do is keep his ears open and his mouth shut.'

With the first lot of buildings completed, the grounds had to be developed. Bob was intoxicated by the possibilities and worked every daylight hour.

'Will you put down that tree and stop this nonsense,' I said. 'Even the boys warn you to rest in the middle of the day. You could at least wear a hat. I'm not talking about what the Balinese say about a white man working like a coolie. I'm only thinking about your health.'

'Will you stop fussing,' Bob said. 'I feel fine.'

The landscape gardening progressed rapidly with women bringing coral for the paths and men dragging in carts of rich earth for borders and flowerbeds. With no regard for face, Bob could not resist working with them. He even inspired our jongoses to pitch in and help although they normally considered such work beneath them. Nothing could stop Bob until he came down again with malaria.

Though he was even sicker than the first time, he refused Dr Roestam's advice to go to hospital, but he did agree to go to Dr Roestam's house. I took him to Denpasar, a blanket over his pyjamas, while he babbled in unrelated sentences. Dr and Mrs Roestam put him in bed in their guest room and stationed a boy outside his room, day and night, to attend to him. I slept in the room on a chaise longue. Three times a day we were served European meals although the Roestams ate Javanese food in mid-morning and late afternoon.

When we left, five days later, I tried to pay Dr Roestam for their hospitality but he said sternly, 'Guests in my house do not pay anything. It is not the custom of our country.' We tried to make up for it later by getting him medical books he wanted from the United States.

In our absence, Rankop and Tampa had been able to hold the four guests we had left behind, partly because I had given Rankop a fair idea of a balanced diet. He was ambitious, highly strung and eager to handle the meals with as little interference from me as possible. At times he declared his independence by changing my menus a little even if it meant more work for him.

In spite of frequent skirmishes, we developed good team-work. If a car full of people arrived unexpectedly, I would hurry to Denpasar in a dogcart to shop while Rankop whipped up a meal with whatever we had. Never in all our years in Bali did he lose his head during emergencies, and only a tight, nervous cough showed his tension. Coping with breakfast orders when everyone wanted something different was especially trying. When the work threatened to submerge him, he coughed and his eyes shone like those of a firehorse in harness.

After that first enforced absence during Bob's bout of malaria, I never worried about being away for a few days. In the beginning, though, every meal needed criticism. Some mistakes were mortifying. Why not cover grilled tenderloin with a fish gravy? What could be wrong with serving cold oatmeal — so like corn starch pudding — with fruit sauce as a dessert? How was it possible to keep ants and cockroaches out of the palm sugar syrup which we used on pancakes?

After every meal I went to the kitchen to discuss the courses with as much praise as possible. At times I sent notes in Malay from the dining room as encouragement. Later on I wrote them in English, which he was learning, or in Balinese, which I was learning. His notes to me were often illustrated with drawings of legendary figures. We entertained each other.

Learning about the Balinese

We did not know how to organise more than two servants, and the problem became acute when we found no regular days off were possible. Instead of one day off a week, each boy returned to his village for celebrations occurring at odd times.

'We're having trouble with your days off,' I said to Rankop and Tampa as they sat cross-legged on the floor, peeling shrimps. This subject was always difficult, so Rankop's expression became sullen and Tampa lost his smile.

'You both live so far away, you leave for four days at a time. The others have only two days off, as is the custom. I know it takes you half a day on the bus to get to Bangli but now we have many guests. We never know when more will arrive. What are your thoughts?'

'I have already thought,' Rankop said, a sly smile creeping through his automatic resentment. 'I have rented ground in the village behind. I am buying bamboo to make a house. My wife and baby will live there.'

'So that's why you have been going off on your bicycle so often. Does your wife want to come here?'

'I've told her she's coming to live in Kuta. Perhaps she wants to.'

'How about you, Tampa? Could you live here and not go home so often? Perhaps you will get married soon? Maybe there is a girl

in Kuta you like — you stay so long when you go to market?'

'I have no girl,' he said, turning away with a dark blush on his light skin. If he did not have one he was surely looking. The market is a good place to meet women as buying is a chance to flirt. Other chances could arise at the ceremonies and other gatherings

↟ Dutch officials and their wives sit in the background at an aristocratic religious occasion. The Balinese often could not understand the status enjoyed by European women, who were even permitted to sit with men at meals.

where girls sold food from little stalls. Respectable girls did not wander out alone but selling was different. It kept them too busy to get into trouble.

Rankop built a little house with two rooms and installed his wife and baby. Then Tampa married and built a house next to Rankop's. I visited the two houses occasionally and found them always neat and clean. The boys had adopted some of our ways. Instead of sleeping on mat-covered slats and dirty pillows, they had thick mattresses, white sheets and pillow cases.

Both decorated their walls with photographs cut from magazines and bad paintings I had discarded. Tampa added frills by hanging burned-out electric light bulbs from coloured ribbons, festooning the walls with red and blue paper streamers and covering his packing case bureau with a tie-and-dye cloth which was almost hidden under photographs guests had given him of himself and the rest of the staff.

All this time we were learning about the Balinese. There were about one and a quarter million of them, and with modern disease control their number was increasing rapidly. Most lived in the southern part of the island, the central and northern parts being too mountainous for much rice farming. Only the western part, covered with thick, low jungle where hunters said they could still find tigers, remained to take care of the overflowing population.

The Dutch colonial government of the island was lenient as a result of bitter lessons learned in Java and in the Dutch campaigns to take over Bali. Every effort was made to interfere as little as possible with the people's way of life. The highest authority on the island was the Resident of Bali and Lombok, an officer who lived in north Bali and who was responsible to the Governor-General of the Dutch East Indies in Batavia. There was an Assistant Resident in the south, in Denpasar, and then eight Controleurs, one for each of the island's eight rajas. Beneath this overall Dutch control, the system of government still ran from the rajas down through village councils to the people.

Partly for historical reasons, partly because Bali did not have much to exploit — it had only a small export trade in rice, pigs and coffee — the Dutch treated the Balinese better than they did the Javanese. High caste Balinese were treated almost as equals. But it would be an exaggeration to say the lower classes were respected. They had equal rights with any white man before the law but were looked on as inferiors in every other way.

Yet they were not ordered about with the sharpness prevailing in Java. Even the Resident would have found difficulty in keeping servants had he done so. The wife of a newly arrived Controleur told me she had been mystified at being unable to hold a cook or a houseboy until she found that she must not handle them autocratically.

In general the Balinese are a carefree people — but they rear their own children very strictly. From babyhood children are trained to accept life's obligations and limitations, to control their emotions and to abide by time-honoured rules. Like all children they crave attention and affection, but soon find they are being brought up more by their own generation than by their parents.

Because of this, they learn to observe others' rights at an early

▲ Children 'play' by imitating their elders at work, as when they offer snacks for sale. They have virtually no toys.

age, and to suppress desire for close relationships for the rest of their lives. They abandon all hope of being indulged and derive their play satisfaction from imitating their elders in light forms of work and, vicariously, from the frequent dramas, dances, shadow plays and temple ceremonies.

A girl of six starts to develop the straight back and fine carriage of her race by carrying light loads on her head when accompanying her mother along the road. A boy of six may drive water buffalo to their daily bath or help his grandfather usher the ducks home at night from the flooded ricefields. Babies are carried to all-night entertainments while children old enough to run about are given the front row in the audience.

I saw no toys except an occasional bird on a string, and only infrequently did I see a group playing some childish game. I gained the impression that the earliest activities were a direct preparation for adult life. A small girl would tend an even smaller child all day, playing nursemaid while the boys were watching and imitating manly activities.

The resultant precociousness is not followed by child marriages, however. Among the high castes marriages may be arranged and a

▲ Small girls look after their younger brothers and sisters, and also quickly learn to carry headloads. Taking offerings to temple is part of every Balinese girl's upbringing.

The dying legong

A touching chapter in one of our guest's many months with us was his devotion to three girls aged eight, nine and ten. As they were legong dancers, performers of Bali's most famous dance, he was able to see them often by persuading new arrivals to engage their company.

After each performance the three dignified children, shimmering in stiff, gold costumes and winged helmets, took turns sitting on our guest's lap, holding his hand and smiling at him without words. Sometimes they covered his curly red hair with a solid cap of blossoms from their helmets, tearing him between pleasure at the experience and unease at the spectacle he presented.

I was glad he left before we knew that Munik, the youngest and sweetest, was seriously ill. All three posed for me often, staying a week each time and sleeping in the extra room behind the office. They were docile little birds, accepting silently what Rankop gave them to eat and working for me for hours on end. If I needed only one, the other two had to be there for fear of missing something. Like all Balinese dancing children, they were not afraid of strangers. They sat with our guests, sipping lemonade, or danced a turn for them without any coy protests.

Munik declined gradually. Breathing became hard and sweat broke out on her face after the least effort. She became thinner and more transparent. When Bob took her to the hospital, we discovered that she had a congenital heart disease and could not live more than a few months more.

'She won't last long in her village,' the doctor said. 'She would be better off here or with you.'

'We'll take care of her if her family agree,' Bob said. 'But I'm sure they won't like the idea.'

'We have a high caste male nurse here,' the doctor said. 'I'll have him talk to the parents. The Balinese put a lot of stock in what a high caste says.'

The parents were frozen at the news but, believing the nurse, were persuaded to turn Munik over to us. We asked only that they did not bring food when they visited her. We wanted her to have the most vitamin-rich diet possible, with milk and cod liver oil every day.

When she arrived, I sent for kettles of hot water and gave her the first warm bath she would ever have had. I washed her hair and dressed her in clean sarong and blouse.

'You must take a bath every day,' I said, 'and put on clean

clothes. Give Made Pinatou the clothes you take off. We'll help you wash your hair once a week.'

A few days later I reminded Munik that she had not taken a bath or changed her clothes since she arrived. She was puzzled. 'It's because we haven't had a holiday yet,' she said seriously.

She spent the mornings sitting behind the kitchen, talking to the boys, who, like all Balinese, were kind and gentle with children, or watching the girls from Kuta selling cigarettes and packets of sweetened rice or coconut behind the garage. She lay on her bed most of the afternoon and sat with us in the evenings, when I carried her back and forth.

Only rest could add a few weeks to her life. Her angelic face and gentle manners, her satisfaction with the little pleasures left her, were tragic to us. As I held her in my lap, her body shook with the pounding of her enlarged heart.

Twice a week, her parents, the other two girls and the manager of her dance group came to see her. After six weeks, her feet began to swell — a sign of the end. When we told her parents what the symptoms meant, they asked to take her back to their traditional doctor as a last resort. We knew that the strenuous life of the village would allow her only a few more days of life, but it seemed better for her to be with her own people.

Seven days later, a messenger from her village arrived. We knew what he had to say.

'We should give a cloth to wrap her in,' Leekas said.

I imagined ten guilders would be enough for a shroud, but asked his opinion.

'For a child of her station, one guilder,' Leekas said. A poor end to so sweet a scrap of humanity.

Her parents came to thank us for our care, bringing fruit and eggs, as they had so many times before. They sat speechless and

miserable. Bob went to the dining room and took an enlarged photograph of Munik from the wall. It showed her with the honeyed smile of the dance, her slender figure swayed back, her arms raised, one hand holding a fan, the other bent like a curved . leaf. Her mother took it with tears starting from her eyes. Nothing was said. After a few moments of polite delay, her parents walked slowly down the driveway, carrying the photograph.

pre-adolescent girl may be married to a boy she has never seen before. But other people allow their children to make their own choices. Girls are not married until they are sixteen or more and boys do not attempt marriage until they are old enough to take on responsibility for a wife and children.

In general the Dutch have interfered very little with the Balinese way of life, or their religion, which amount to the same thing. Everything they do is part of their religious life. While we were in Bali a few Christian missionaries were at work there, but they were supposed not to make new converts. They were expected to be careful — especially as an early missionary had been murdered when his only convert found himself an outcast among his own people. He hired assassins to remove the menace. But there were Balinese Christians and they did not come under such control as the missionaries did.

One day one of them approached Leekas (about whom more later) with a proposition. If he preached the Christian gospel, he would get twenty guilders a month. Leekas, knowing nothing of Christianity, asked how he would know what to say.

'I'll tell you,' the convert said. 'You talk so well, you can convince people.'

Leekas needed money badly but refused the job because he did not want to preach something he did not believe in and because 'my old mother would have died if I had done such a thing'. Money was not that important, he told me.

One day I was able to show an American dentist, Edwin Hobart, a ceremony heavily laden with culture and religion which also drew his professional interest. He had heard of Balinese teeth-filing and wondered if he could see such an occasion. We found one for him. Two adolescent girls of a well-to-do Denpasar family were to be filed while hundreds of people were entertained to a feast.

We found them sitting on a bed in their house, in ceremonial dress, limp and frightened, while elderly women painted and powdered their faces, fastened gold flowers in their hair and slipped on gold bracelets and anklets.

'It can't be true,' Dr Hobart said, 'that these children are voluntarily going to have their teeth wrecked.'

'Indeed they are,' I said, explaining that every Balinese has his or her teeth filed into an even line soon after puberty, or as soon after that as his family can afford the entertainment that goes with the ceremony. The object is to rescue a person from looking like an animal and therefore running the risk of being treated as one when seeking a place in heaven. Filing also reduces a person's liability to animal passions. No connection is seen between exposing the dentine of the teeth and later decay.

'Can't the government stop it?' Dr Hobart asked.

'It could,' I said, 'but it makes a point of not interfering with Balinese customs. It doesn't even object to corpses being kept in a village for months, awaiting cremation. You've already noticed that many old people have only rotting stumps where their upper front teeth used to be. But if the government started tampering with these things, the Balinese would soon have nothing to live for. Religion and culture are interlocked. If you attack any part, you threaten the whole.'

In a pavilion a priest waited, standing beside an earthen pot from which protruded three large mechanic's files such as you might find in a motor workshop. One of the two girls was carried to the pavilion and laid on a silk-covered mattress so her head fell back over the edge.

After intoning a brief prayer, the priest took one of the files and began to grind away at the girl's upper teeth. Dr Hobart got so close he could see every detail. After a few minutes a relative took over the filing. A chorus of women sang a monotonous dirge.

'She can take it,' Dr Hobart commented. 'Look at the tears rolling down her temples. But she doesn't make a sound.'

After twenty minutes the girl was allowed to sit up and look in a mirror. Shaking her head, she threw herself back for more. When she was finally satisfied, she walked off as if nothing had happened. Her sister took her place.

Not only Balinese adolescents had their teeth filed. During a visit to a small guesthouse in the mountains, we were introduced to Alex, an English planter from South Africa, and Kitty, a tall American woman who wrote travel books. Both were in full Balinese regalia — a little self-conscious but pleased with themselves.

'You should have been here the other day,' Kitty said. 'We had a real teeth-filing ceremony. Don't you think Alex's teeth look beautiful? Show them, Alex.'

There was no doubt about it. Alex's upper teeth were as straight across as if they had been sliced off with a knife.

'He had the whole performance,' Kitty said. 'He had a priest and a chorus of singing women. We decorated everything and we had duck and roast pig for about a hundred people. There was an orchestra and a shadow play and an opera performance. Alex feels like a real Balinese now, don't you, Alex?'

The star of the occasion squirmed uneasily, and suddenly leaned forward.

'You may laugh,' he said, 'but these people have something we lack. Even if they are superstitious and live in fear of gods and demons, at least they're not hampered by our civilisation. They really enjoy life, make a good time out of what little they have. I'd like to be one of them. Perhaps I made a fool of myself, but then . . '

'Do you think you could ever belong?' I asked. 'Wouldn't you always be the white tuan, always playing a part?'

'Yes, I guess I would,' he said, reaching out to stroke the arm of a village girl kneeling on the grass by his chair. 'But I'm on holiday, and I'm having a damn good time.'

European visitors have been inclined to romanticise Bali, and to say that the Balinese have the secret of harmony and contentment. They claim that a complete escape from the problems of civilisation and the inner conflict worrying most of us can be achieved by settling down in Bali, as if some soothing spirit would enter the distressed soul or as if happiness were catching.

They do not stop to realise that the serenity of the Balinese is assured by a culture completely wrapped in religious beliefs and social customs. These give answers to all problems — but they are answers satisfactory only to a people sheltered from contact with the outer world. For an outsider to find in Bali a lasting substitute for his former way of life, purposeful activity beyond the limits of native life is essential. A person capable of such activity could be happy anywhere.

The following chapter is about three people who came to Bali seeking happiness, and about three totally different results.

Three foreigners

We followed a wooded path into a densely covered arbor thick with orange lilies and jonquils. A square clearing was covered with lattices heavy with bougainvillea and morning glories. Furnished with bamboo chairs, it was an outdoor sitting room, wrapped in soft green light. Steps at one side led up to the stained wood porch of a thatched cottage.

A tall young woman came sedately towards us. Her smooth, brown body, clothed only in a sarong, was broad shouldered and narrow hipped. Her breasts floated in vigorous curves. Her face had the dignity of a Greek marble, with large eyes and sensual but clean-cut lips. Her black hair was brushed back and her pierced earlobes were distended with gold plugs. She would have been a sensation in any drawing room, in any kind of clothes.

M. le Meyeur de Merpres (the man who discomfitted Mr Smit) must be a fine man to hold the loyalty of such a prize, I thought. She was Polok, by far the most beautiful Balinese woman I had seen. She told us le Meyeur was riding a pony on the beach and would be back soon, and left.

We sat smoking and speculating about her life. Then about twenty, she had been posing for le Meyeur for years, and had been to Singapore with him to help sell his paintings by performing Balinese dances. In her day she had been the most famous legong dancer on the island. The artist, already elderly, had carried her off to his arbored cottage in Sanur, and married her in a Balinese ceremony.

He had given her rich clothes, gold jewellery and even a private bathroom with white tiles. When he died he would leave everything to her. She had security and no doubt helped her family. But it was a far cry from the life she must have known before. Perhaps she had not wanted to become the wife of a Balinese man.

In that role she would have been a servant in her own home, she would not be allowed to eat with her husband, or walk along the street with him, or speak to him in public unless it were really necessary. Even her children would not belong to her. She could be divorced at her husband's whim but could not free herself from him unless he behaved outrageously. Perhaps she had weighed all these things before accepting le Meyeur. Although the Balinese do not have an understanding of romantic love as we know it, perhaps she valued what was undoubtedly deep and unselfish adoration.

A sturdy, elderly man with grey hair and a kind, wrinkled face rode through a narrow break in the hedge hiding the beach. He jumped off as a boy ran up to lead his pony away. We introduced ourselves, and he invited us on to his porch. Despite being crowded with European furniture, it had the feeling of Bali. Posts and beams were carved with flower and fruit designs and some of le Meyeur's paintings hung on the wall.

His pictures were not so much of Bali as of the artist's dream life. Slender, broad shouldered maidens sat in flower sprinkled meadows under Japanese parasols against tender yellow and green lights. Rose and golden green predominated in an unreal world of freely rendered figures in indistinct settings, flooded with light, harmony and peace. The paint was wiped on with broad sweeps. Le Meyeur painted Polok morning and afternoon, producing enough paintings to have an exhibition in Singapore every two years.

He took us from one room to another through gold, carved doors. His paintings were everywhere. Big white beds with mosquito nets filled the bedrooms. The kitchen was immaculate with glistening white tiles. We sat on stiff chairs around a lace covered table in an indoor sitting room while Polok brought glasses of arak

➤ *Dancers entertain in the hotel grounds — one of Bob's photographs . . .*

127

seasoned with spices and orange peel. Bob, as one builder and gardener to another, complimented le Meyeur on his beautiful home.

'I've added slowly to the house and garden through the years,' he said. 'I'm glad you like it. I hope you can come again. It's impossible for me to get out much as I paint most of the time,

. . . and one of my paintings.

although Polok and I go to Denpasar once a week in our dogcart, shopping.'

When I asked about cooking, hoping for useful hints, he said that Polok was a wonderful cook. 'She has several helpers, but she's the boss.'

'I noticed your fine brick altar near the arbor,' I said. 'It's for Polok, I suppose?'

'We're very pleased with it,' he responded enthusiastically. 'The top stone was carved by a real artist. Polok makes her offerings there.'

After that we often met le Meyeur and his fairytale princess in Denpasar or at some temple celebration. She was the embodiment of every man's dreams, and it seemed to me that le Meyeur had achieved the ultimate in romance.

Paul Napier (not his real name) was the exact opposite. His life was most complicated. He was always in a dither, always hours late, always trying to figure out how to sell another picture, or how to get another paying guest for his little house in the mountains. He was an enthusiastic drinker, and as a result his naturally plump figure was even plumper. He was always running his fingers through disordered grey hair in a frenzied effort to collect his wits.

The first time we met Paul, he was sitting in his garden with two of his boarders and several pretty village girls. Surprisingly, the girls were not chaperoned. He was said to have ridden all over Bali on his bicycle, when he was fitter, sampling its female offerings. I wondered about this because Balinese women are not that easy.

Paul showed us through his house. Everything was in a state of turmoil. The rooms were full of half finished paintings, artist's materials and frames. Balinese paintings were tacked to the walls and carvings filled the corners. Paul's own work vaguely resembled Gaugin's.

We saw his collection of Balinese pornography, ink and water-colour representations of men with enlarged organs about to have intercourse with women and animals. The Balinese have no word for this — such things are simply funny. Paul sold items from his collection (discreetly, since it was illegal) along with other 'bargains' he obtained through his 'exclusive knowledge of the island'. Always parting with them, of course, at great sacrifice.

At times he sold as antiques, for twenty guilders or more, carvings which could be bought in Denpasar for a guilder each. He also made several hundred percent profit on batiks which he bought in Denpasar for perhaps two guilders each, claiming to have got them from distant sources known only to him.

One of his guests asked my opinion of some batiks she was considering buying from Paul. She told me his price. I showed her duplicates in an Indian shop in Denpasar. Paul stopped speaking to us, which we did not much regret.

Paul also claimed to know where to find 'secret ceremonies' and 'unique erotic dances' in villages which only he and his friends could enter. Gullible tourists fell for his line when he said he would take them there as a special favour. They were not to know that he knew no more secrets than did any other informed outsider, or that he would have them spend days visiting each of several places which in fact were close to each other, or that he charged fifty percent more for using his car than the standard rate.

Months after we first met Paul, he enthralled some of our guests by arranging a barong dance, in which men in self-induced trances try to stab themselves in the chests with krisses. Our guests told us that the performance was especially for Paul and that he was the only person who could arrange it 'out of season'. The Balinese believed he had a magic power to hold in check the evil spirits called forth during the dance, they said. The price had been high — but little for such a privilege.

There would have been no point in trying to tell them the truth, in deflating their excitement. The barong dance in fact is thrilling and it would be a shame to ruin their impression of it. And had we tried to tell them that a barong dance can be arranged at small cost on almost any day of the year, they might have disbelieved us and thought us guilty of trying to discredit a competitor.

Not long afterwards we received a letter from a tourist who had met our earlier guests. 'Would you try to find us one of those amazing kris dances, called barong, that occur twice a year?' he wrote. 'Perhaps one might be performed during our stay. Never mind the expense, so long as you manage to get us in.'

He and his friends arrived, they saw one of the best barong

dances, enjoyed it immensely, and paid the usual very low fee.

Like Paul, Miss Anna Bleecher (not her real name) exploited Bali's attractions at times in devious ways. She claimed to have been converted to the Balinese religion, and had adorned her property with altars where she placed offerings when tourists arrived. Her buildings were surrounded by a huge stone wall and hidden from each other by masses of banana trees. To the unknowing the place reeked of glamour and mystery.

Mrs Faucet, one of our guests, met Anna at a dance and returned to say her new friend had offered to build her a cheap studio where she could live and paint during the two years she expected to be in Bali. Mrs Faucet would pay the cost, which Anna would return gradually by providing free meals and room service. Since I wished Mrs Faucet well, I warned her to watch her purse. Incensed at my aspersion, she left without a word of farewell.

Six weeks later she walked into our studio, one of her paintings under her arm, spluttering with rage.

'Can you put me up?' she asked.

'Of course. What happened?'

'Never in my life have I had such an experience,' she said. 'I've been put out! Thrown out! Cheated! Robbed! Yesterday my studio was completed. When I suggested moving in, Anna told me she refused to serve me any more meals. Just like that. For the past week she hasn't spoken to me, for no reason that I know of. Every night I've heard strange rappings on my roof with queer lights and howling at the windows. I'm a nervous wreck. Something sinister is going on in that place.'

Mrs Faucet settled in with us, and then went to the Controleur in Denpasar to put in a claim for the money she had lost.

'What proof have you?' he asked.

'These receipts,' she said.

'But these aren't proof of anything. Miss Bleecher has received certain sums from you for a studio — but there is no mention of what studio or for whom. Have you no contract?'

'No,' Mrs Faucet answered dolefully. 'I trusted Miss Bleecher. She was so good to me at first. When I suggested we have a written agreement she said we didn't need one between good friends. She said it in such a way that I was ashamed of my suggestion.'

'When did you first sense trouble coming?'

'A week ago. Miss Bleecher told me she had heard from an American artist who was coming to Bali and wanted a studio. After that moment she never spoke to me again, and sent my meals on a tray so I've been entirely alone. It's all coming to me gradually. I've been too upset to think straight. But now I see that she realised she could get my studio for nothing — or she may have planned it from the first. Of course, all the goings on at night and shoving my meals at me on a tray were part of a campaign to force me to leave. Surely you can do something for me?'

'I'm very sorry. I can do nothing for you without documentary proof.'

Mrs Faucet stayed with us for four months, and never recovered from the shock. The financial loss was serious as she had only a small income, but the deceit had hurt her even more. Occasionally she drove past Anna's house and saw her studio through the open gateway, well lit and obviously occupied.

Tourists range from hard-boiled realists who want everything proved to those whose hunger for sensation makes them believe everything they are told. There are not many at this second extreme — but enough to support racketeers all over the world. We had a ringside seat from which to study the techniques used to fool the unwary, and we were angered and humiliated.

The honest ones among those in Bali who supported themselves by serving tourists could make a reasonable living without misrepresentation. They could realise a fair return by selling native art products for what they really were. They did not find it necessary to claim that any villages or dances were 'secret' or 'exclusive'. Bali's offerings are sufficiently rewarding without this sort of overdressing.

As a tourist, if you are predominantly realistic, you will probably not be fooled. If you are predominantly emotional, you will surely be fooled if you do not take the trouble to check on anyone who offers you the 'secrets' and 'treasures' of any country. Once captured by the black magic of manufactured glamour, you are lost, at least for a time, along with your dignity.

$\mathcal{A}$ refrigerator, a car, a celebration

We had a series of delightful guests from all over the world. In no other way could we have met such a variety of people. Our only regret, in those early days, was that we could not give them the meals they deserved because we did not have enough money for a refrigerator. Nyepi, New Year's Day, a day of silence and inactivity, brought home this disadvantage most forcefully.

'We may not cook tomorrow and we may not use lamps,' Rankop said.

I asked what we could give the guests to eat. Without ice we could not keep anything overnight.

'I can cook vegetables for salad,' Rankop said. 'Maybe they will keep. We can open ham and corned beef. But for breakfast we cannot make good coffee, and we can't cook toast or eggs. Will the guests be angry?'

'No, I will explain to them.'

Nyepi is devoted to exorcising devils — a kind of spring house-cleaning. On the first day, big temple celebrations entertain the gods. When all are assembled, the bad as well as the good, the priests drive out the bad with powerful spells. The children help by parading through the streets shouting and banging tin cans or anything else that makes a noise. Cockfights are held everywhere for blood sacrifices. Brilliantly dressed processions marched from Denpasar to the beach, past our hotel, for ceremonies at a coral temple nearby.

But the second day was one of quiet. No fires, no cooking, no work, no transport of any kind. A driver of a car breaking the rule would have to pay a fine to the local district government.

'What do the Balinese do for rice?' I asked Rankop. 'If you keep cooked rice overnight it turns sour.'

'Yes, it turns sour but we still eat it.'

I told our guests about the coming discomfort, about how they could have only cold food all day, and would have to go to bed soon after sunset or sit in the dark. Even flashlights were not permitted. They were undismayed. All they asked was a trip by car, for which they would gladly pay the five guilders fine.

The next morning we breakfasted on fruit juice, lukewarm coffee from a defective thermos flask, and bread and butter. For lunch we had a salad I shall never forget for everything in it was a little off — not exactly decayed but on the wrong side. What dinner would be like after a few more hours of festering I did not like to think.

That afternoon we all went to Tafelhoek, the rugged, barren peninsula at Bali's southern tip. There, high above sweeping lines of breakers that seem to be held back by a slow-motion camera, stands the temple of Uluwatu, right on the edge of the cliff. Its gates of grey stone suggest the passing of centuries, but most temples in Bali have a timeworn look after a few years because the volcanic building stone is so soft. They are cheerfully patched and rebuilt because time is the cheapest of all commodities and nothing is expected to be permanent.

As we drove back, bumping slowly over the grass-grown road of rocks and ruts, we could see the 'neck' of south Bali spread out beneath us, our beach curving to the west, Kuta behind it, the shallow harbour of Benoa, which only small ships can enter, to the east. The island of Nusa Penida lay further to the east, and northwards, in the clear, amber light, the mountains of Bali rose in straight-edged cones. Mount Agung, the home of the gods, towered above them all.

As we drove through Kuta village, a few lamps shone in the shabby Chinese shops. If the law were so easily broken, could we modify our intended blackout? I asked Rankop what the Chinese, who were always on such good terms with the Balinese, were doing with lights. He thought Kuta might be an exception to the rule, and that perhaps we too might break it without causing ill-will.

We lit our lamps and the cooks whipped up a very decent meal.

Within six months of opening our hotel earned its first modern improvements.

'We're going to have a refrigerator that makes ice,' I said slowly. It was always fun to impress the Balinese with the achievements of science.

Rankop asked what would make it cold.

'Fire,' I said. 'A kerosene lamp underneath. You will keep it burning all the time. Inside will be ice for the drinks.'

'Fine,' said Rankop, squaring his muscular shoulders but politely concealing his doubts. 'But how does fire make ice?'

I had no idea, so I changed the subject by saying that we would no longer have to throw out all our leftovers.

Excitement mounted for ten days, until a truck drove in with a huge crate. Bob bossed the uncrating, until a shining white case stood naked and glistening against the dark matting walls of the kitchen.

The lighting of the lamp should have been attended by some priestly ritual — for no cold came. Hours elapsed and nothing happened. The only sign of activity was a trickle of smoke from a vent at the back. Bob and I lost so much face that I feared hothing would ever make up for it. Bob left for Denpasar to phone Java and berate the salesman.

After a few more days of face-losing, a mechanic arrived. We turned the refrigerator over while chemicals gurgled through the inner pipes, set it upright, turned it over, set it upright once more. The lamp was lit, the cold came, the mechanic departed, and the refrigerator got warm.

Bob phoned again, angrily — $330 gone and no ice. After ten days of correspondence we were told something might be wrong with the lamp. We were sent another, and The Miracle worked.

At first Tampa and Rankop did not understand what went into the refrigerator and what did not. Meat stood on the counter all night while unopened cans were stored inside. The door was left open. Plates and large bowls filled the space so there was no room for the food. The idea of using the covered glass containers was too revolutionary and they were never used at all.

The lamp was neglected and smoked every few days, so the whole ventilating system had to be taken out and cleaned of soot. Or the oil was forgotten and the lamp went out. Bottles were removed and not replaced so our guests never knew when they were going to get warm beer.

'How many time have I told you . . .' I would explode, on this or that. At times I thought my disposition had been permanently ruined. Losing your temper is a serious breach of good manners in Balinese eyes. They call it 'wind in the head'. You should be self-controlled and polite at all times. Harsh words should be saved for very serious occasions and then followed by a smile.

In the end, the technique of managing a refrigerator was mastered, more or less, and the result was a vast difference in economy, comfort and the quality of our meals.

Our next most pressing need was a car.

'Have located secondhand Ford $250 condition questionable all others too expensive wire opinion.'

Bob's telegram was from Surabaya, where he had earlier learned that a new car cost exactly double the retail price in the US and that even secondhand ones were expensive for what you got. Our limit was $250, but we had to buy. Shopping in a dogcart was wearing me out and Bob felt like a prisoner.

'Rely on your judgement,' was all I could answer.

A few days later, a snorting rattle, a screeching of brakes and a call, 'Hello! Where are you?'

I ran out, looked, and exclaimed, 'What a wreck!' A rash of paint on rusty tin, ugly stains on the canvas top and stuffing bursting out of the upholstery.

'Jump in,' Bob said, aglow with excitement. 'See how well it runs. It made the trip beautifully.' He was so pleased he did not notice my disappointment.

We took the road to Denpasar, always severely corrugated. The rattle of the engine, violent bumps and teeth chattering vibration were such that we could only laugh and be thankful that the engine and brakes worked. In a few minutes I began to appreciate our new blessing as I saw the ricefields whizzing by. I decided that when I went to town on errands I would take any guests with me who had endurance and no pride. If they did not like it, well, they could hire a good car and pay the price.

Our horizons broadened at once. We had wings, even if they were those of a moth-eaten bat. Ownership of a refrigerator and a car made us socially expansive. Rejoicing took the form of our first real dinner party.

We were planning an evening's entertainment for the Dewa Agung, the most senior raja in Bali, and a lesser raja, and we needed a good gamelan orchestra. That of X village was one of the best, and had excellent kebyar and legong dancers.

'Can you play for us in four days' time?' Bob asked the headman.

'We cannot play in four days,' he replied, eyes on the ground.

'Can you in five days?' Bob asked.

'We cannot.'

'When can you play for us?'

'We cannot play for you.'

'Why not?'

'Maybe we can play but we have to ask Nyonya Z first.'

'You have to ask Nyonya Z? What has she to say about your playing for us or anyone else?'

'Nyonya forbids us to play for you.'

Bob looked at me in astonishment. This white woman with such influence must have something against us. Perhaps she resented us as newcomers.

'Please go to see Nyonya Z,' Bob said calmly to the headman, who was shifting from one foot to the other. 'I'll come back this afternoon to hear the news.'

'Admirable self-control,' I said as we left. 'I know it was the only way, but I would have lost my temper. But in case they can't be persuaded, we had better try Mario. Let's run up to Tabanan and see him now.'

Mario, the best male dancer in Bali, had been classed by professional dancers visiting Bali as among the world's finest. If we could get him we would have our party set.

But in Tabanan it was the same story. Mario, his mobile face suddenly forlorn, said he was not dancing, he was too busy, he did not feel well.

'I believe I see the same hand here,' I said to Bob. 'Mario certainly can't afford to refuse engagements, and he looks in the best

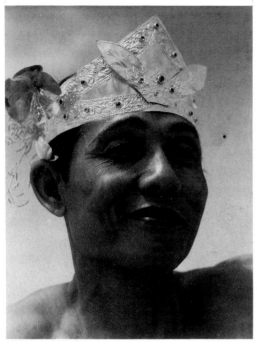

of health. If we don't break this now it may spread. Let's ask him to go with us to see the Raja. He lives close by.'

Mario willingly accompanied us to the palace of polished tile floors and carved wood pillars and thatch more than a foot thick. The Raja, a wide-faced and stocky man in brown sarong, white shirt and dark sack coat, asked us to sit on his porch and called for lemon pop. When we had told him our trouble, he offered to speak to Mario alone. They walked off together. After a few minutes the Raja returned alone.

'Mario is afraid to dance for you. He says Nyonya Z has forbidden him to do so. She told him that if he did no other white person would engage him again.'

'Is that not bad custom?' Bob asked. 'Mario does not belong to Nyonya Z. He must be free to dance for anyone who pays him and treats him well. I can give him much work. Most of my guests will want to see him. Nyonya Z did not tell the truth when she said that dancing for me would hurt him.'

'I shall try to help you,' the Raja said.

Back at X village, when we returned, the headman told us he had been unable to find Nyonya Z.

'You are starting a bad custom,' Bob said. 'You are throwing away work. Our guests pay to see entertainments. If you will not play for us now, I shall never ask you again.'

'We haven't the courage,' the headman said, looking alarmed.

▲ *Mario, one of the finest dancers in the world.*

We knew he was an enterprising bargainer for his troupe, so the pressure on him had to be severe.

Bob asked him to think carefully because there would not be another time.

'There is another reason,' the headman added hurriedly. 'You know we play often for the Bali Hotel. The manager also forbids us to play for you.'

'That I just don't believe,' Bob said, trying to suppress real alarm. 'Come on,' he said to me. 'We'll go straight to see him.'

'Absolutely untrue,' the manager stated. 'I won't have that kind of thing going on. I'll send for the headman at once to get to the bottom of this. He may not use my name in making up such stories. I'll tell him that if he wants to play for me, he must play for everyone who wishes to engage him. If you go to see him tomorrow, I think you'll find everything cleared up.'

The next day the headman was unctuous one minute, cool the next. He felt himself under an obligation to Nyonya Z but could not afford to lose the patronage of the Bali Hotel. He was torn by some feud he could not understand. Hesitantly, he agreed that his gamelan would play in four days' time.

'Leni,' I said to one of our guests, a Dutch woman. 'I hope you won't mind if the rajas are served first at dinner. Our boys have been trained to serve the women first but they tell me they haven't the courage to do it tonight. You know how they feel about their rajas. They prostrate themselves in their presence.'

She hesitated. 'If that's the right thing to do, that's all right with me, although I think the rajas should be taught some manners.'

'They have all the manners you could ask for, only different from ours. Their wives don't rate, you know. They take them to official receptions and dinners because it's expected by the Dutch, but you can imagine how they must scorn our practice of allowing women to eat in mixed company. It's heresy.'

The Dewa Agung arrived dressed in blue and gold headcloth, a blue and gold kain panjang (a cloth extending from waist to knees and then falling in folds to the floor), a short black jacket and sandals. He was a heavy, middle-aged man with the manner of one used to homage. The Raja with him was similarly dressed and equally untalkative. They drank brem, a rice wine, while the rest of

Mario dances

One evening we took a party of tourists to Tabanan, where Mario, the most famous dancer in Bali, had agreed to dance for us. We were escorted to a newly built bamboo arbor, canopied with layers of coconut leaves and decorated with flowers, leaves and streamers. The gold, carved gamelan of Tabanan, which had won so many prizes, was at one end, its musicians dressed in blue, red and gold. Mario sat in a corner, his legs crossed under a magenta cloth, his torso wrapped tightly in yellow, a gilt crown on his head.

I marvelled at Balinese acceptance of great artistic gifts. Here was an outstanding artist accorded no more importance in his community than any tiller of the soil. He had a humble job in the Controleur's office in Tabanan (once he gave me a lecture on how to use a telephone), he received a pittance for his dancing, and he was paid nothing, or at most a few sheaves of rice, for his teaching. The only deference I ever saw him receive was from a high caste pupil who sat on the floor with him, as an equal, instead of on a chair.

Our guests, looking upon Mario as they would upon a great performer in their own countries, had once tried to persuade him to have lunch with us. After long urging, he consented, only to sit on the edge of his chair in obvious discomfort. He looked suspiciously at the first course, and cast his eyes about as if about to take flight. A waiter leaned over and said in a low voice, 'Be careful, Mario. Don't stick the fork in your eye.' He dissolved in wriggling laughter.

'You prefer Balinese food?' I asked, taking pity on him. 'Perhaps you want to eat in the back?'

He looked at me gratefully and fled.

That evening in Tabanan, he was to demonstrate how he had turned the kebyar, a dry, traditional dance from north Bali, into something original and individual. At first he danced it throughout in a crosslegged position but through the years he introduced variations, and before we left he was dancing part of it on his feet.

He sat facing us across the trompong, a long row of brass gongs, like upturned bowls in a frame, holding two silver-banded

sticks. As the music began he straightened up slowly and struck the bowls, listening to the tones. Soon he was playing with the orchestra, his face introspective. Gradually he moved on to full, sweeping gestures, twirling the sticks, striking the bells, and

touching them daintily to stop the resonance. His features lit up, his eyes flashed to this side and that, closed as if in repressed ecstacy, seemed to indicate pain. He smiled and one eyebrow rose playfully as if to say, 'It's only a trick, after all.'

He tossed away his sticks and picked up a fan. With his left hand, between the tips of long-nailed fingers, he picked up his magenta train. With fan fluttering and train swirling, he hopped in a circle, his legs still crossed beneath him. I had seen others dancing 'his' kebyar but this was different. When Mario danced, it was like nothing else in Bali. His style and elegance converted suggestions of eroticism into an intellectual pattern which al-

ways sent delicious thrills up our spines.

Later he demonstrated his teaching. One of his pupils was a boy of seven with black eyes like saucers, rosebud mouth and soft, baby curves. Mario squatted behind him, holding his wrists, im-

prisoning the boy's hips between his thighs, controlling the head with his chin. He seemed to encompass the child, absorb him, so as to pass on every movement and expression.

He grasped the pupil's head and jerked it from side to side, put his hand under the pupil's buttocks and jounced him up and down. Holding one hand, he pulled the pupil in a hopping circle. When the pupil failed some complicated hand movements, Mario completed the rhythms alone while the child, pressed against his chest, watched the arms that took the place of his own, and then imitated them perfectly.

Mario was as splendid a teacher as he was a dancer.

us had cocktails. Leni and some of our Denpasar friends chattered away in Malay while Bob charged into complicated subjects, unaware always of his mistakes, waving his hands when words failed him. The servants crawled about the room with backs bent, making themselves as inconspicuous as possible.

The gamelan was already an hour late. We sent a chauffeur to hurry it along. Eleven of us sat at a long table. Chicken soup was served, and then Balinese food for the rajas and European beef and vegetables for the rest of us. But at 8.30 the gamelan had still not arrived. Perhaps it was not coming. In that case the party would certainly be a failure.

'The chauffeur has some of the musicians in his car,' Bob said excitedly. 'He found them sitting on the side of the road, doing nothing, with the two buses we sent. They said the rest weren't through dinner but we know they don't eat this late. It's a crude case of stalling. I'm going to get things moving.'

At 9.30, three and a half hours late, the buses arrived with Bob guarding their rear. He was worn out. We explained the trouble to the rajas and asked the Dewa Agung to lecture the headman. He might make an impression where no one else could.

While the instruments were being arranged, the headman knelt before the Dewa Agung, listening to a gentle lecture. 'For your own good,' it went, 'you must accept all engagements. . . .' The Dewa Agung was making no impression at all, but seemed to be enjoying himself in his reserved way. Perhaps he was even a little amused at our frustration.

After the show, thirty people squeezed into one bus with their instruments. The second they left empty, after insisting that we provide it. It was their last gesture of defiance. To keep our self-esteem and the respect of our servants (who took a very dim view of the gamelan's conduct), we never gave them another opportunity to play at our hotel. Not even after Nyonya Z left Bali and the headman came to us asking for work.

As for Mario, the most famous of all Bali's artists — not many days later he came to Kuta to apologise. He offered to bring his gamelan from Tambanan to entertain us any evening, free, and to dance for us himself. Quick arrangements were made and he gave a magnificent performance, the first of almost weekly engagements through the years.

Like unruly schoolboys

'Music and dancing with meals,' Bob said. 'Too bad we can't afford to advertise. Wouldn't that knock 'em over?'

Increasing business during our first dry season had registered on our servants' rising spirits as on a fever chart. Occasional bursts of firecrackers and a sudden devotion to music and dancing were among the happier outlets.

Rankop made two bamboo xylophones for himself and Tampa. Other boys beat drums with fluttering rhythms and clashed cymbals made of metal reflectors from small kerosene lamps. Someone invented the clear tone of a triangle by hitting a bottle with a knife. Dishpans were struck with padded mallets for gongs. After the orchestra was partially organised, visiting chauffeurs joined in the practising which filled every free hour. As we sat on the beginning of a lawn, drinking cocktails before dinner, we heard the music from the kitchen porch. At times it sounded like a full gamelan orchestra.

To encourage such good and spontaneous entertainment, we borrowed an angklung set, an archaic form of gamelan made of bamboo, and set its four pieces along one wall of the dining room. From them on, we had music for lunch.

After serving a course, the jongoses rushed to the instruments and the cooks hurried in from the kitchen to join them. Gardeners and chauffeurs helped when they felt like it, making rippling harmonies from the four tones in a minor scale, played rapidly with

two mallets. When one piece was finished, another course was served. The only price was the lack of service for second helpings.

Every night the tables were set out under the coconut trees for dinner. Small lamps with basket shades shed a warm light while stars shone overhead and clouds drifted across the moon. The sound of music came to us through the pound and wash of the breakers.

After dinner, a new boy, Nyong Nyong, danced the baris, a war dance. He wore only a loin cloth with hibiscus flowers set over his

▲ *Nyoman Nyong Nyong, seen here in two renderings, was a lively personality. He starred in an early film about Bali and later struck up a friendship, as one star with another, with Charlie Chaplin during his occasional visits to Bali. But Nyong Nyong made his living as a hotel worker.*

148

ears. The light of a few pressure lamps threw his brown, muscular body into dramatic relief against the ghostly palm trunks. He strutted and leapt, eyes wide, lips pursed. Then he made an elegant gesture, brushing his temple or plucking at his imaginary costume.

Tampa might take a turn with leaves tied to his head, his face smeared grotesquely with flour. He parodied Nyong Nyong, exaggerating, tripping over his feet. A quick change into a sarong with a bath towel around his head, and he did a serious legong with feminine grace and subdued, girlish gestures.

Nyong Nyong was a prima donna. He had been the star of a film made in Bali and its remembered glory still clung to him. Showing off was his breath of life. His attention to clothes spread to the others, and they remembered to put flowers in their headcloths. When none were to be found on the bushes, they used artificial ones from a Japanese shop.

But no one approached Nyong Nyong's style. His sarong always trailed exactly right, his headcloth always swung at a certain angle over one temple with a flower extending the line upwards. His upper garment, supposed to extend from armpits to hips, was draped from his waist as an overskirt, that he might display the unblemished skin of his chest and back.

On holidays, he dressed in melting colours to impress the young women of Kuta who came in numbers to giggle and chat with him as he leaned nonchalantly against a post on the kitchen porch. At other times he experimented with European clothes.

One day, swimming, he rose from a wave with his anatomy intimately revealed in a pair of silk panties from some guest's scrap basket. They were almost invisible when wet. But he so admired the effect, in spite of our taunts, that he wore them in swimming until they gave out.

Even conservative Rankop was carried away by the possibilities. Early one morning I noticed his white shorts looked puckered, and found he was wearing an athletic supporter of wide elastic over them.

'Where did you get that?' I asked, trying to keep a straight face.

'A guest gave it to me,' he said solemnly.

'Why don't you wear it inside?'

'Because if I do it will get dirty.'

'It's not supposed to be seen,' I said, although I knew that this would not matter to him. I knew that the only way to get the supporter off Rankop without causing resentment or loss of face was to take the matter lightly.

'Why don't you show your new belt to Nyonya Number Two (the woman in Number Two cottage)?' I suggested. 'Ask her what she thinks of it.' 'Nyonya Number Two' was Eleanor Landon, about whom more shortly. She had much influence with the boys.

Every hour I looked out to see if Rankop was respectable again. I had to leave it to him. He had to be handled with tact. If I spoke sharply to him when things went wrong, he sassed me back and we glared at each other like fighting cocks. By noon he had given in.

The new passion for clothes made it necessary for us to fine the boys when we caught them wearing shirts while on duty. They preferred them to the orange or yellow shawl-like garments, tied with brightly coloured sashes, which we provided as hotel uniforms. Naughty schoolboys could not have been more difficult. If they went out at night in trousers and felt hats or tropical helmets, that was none of our business.

Sometimes there seemed to be no end to the minor complications our boys could invent.

One morning a gold tooth shone between Tampa's lips as he looked at me expectantly with a pleased grin, waiting for approval.

'Your tooth, Tampa!' I almost shouted. 'What have you done?' We tried so hard to forestall calamities and now Tampa, with a perfect set of beautiful, white teeth, had ruined one with a hideous

gold cap.

'I've just come back from the dentist,' he said, crestfallen. 'Don't you like it?'

'I can't tell you how I feel,' I said. Bob was having breakfast. I asked him to go to the kitchen.

'My God! It's awful!' he said when he came back. 'If Tampa had any idea how grotesque . . . They've probably ruined his tooth. What a thing to do to a handsome boy.'

We went to the kitchen to get the whole story but Tampa had already left on his bicycle.

'Quick,' I said. 'We must follow him in the car.' We picked him up a little way down the road and took him to Denpasar. The 'den-

↑ *Here is Rankop again, with his bicycle. He was earlier encountered, with bicycle, on the front cover of this book, on his way to do up a hotel room.*

tists' there were Chinese cobblers whose shop windows displayed both handmade sandals and false teeth.

'How much of the tooth did you grind off?' we asked.

'Only a little bit on the lower edge,' the man said.

He put Tampa in his ancient dentist's chair, rescued from some junkyard. With the pliers he used to pull nails from shoes, he pinched off the gold cap, which turned out to be no more than a thin foil. Underneath was sticky cement, like chewing gum. The job had cost forty US cents, the price of ruining the tooth had the cap remained.

Tampa reached for a black toothbrush on a strip of moulding against the peeling wall. It had every sign of having been used to blacken shoes and must have been in countless mouths without washing. Before I could stop him, he put the unmentionable thing into his mouth and scrubbed.

'Do you see what I see?' Bob asked, another morning at breakfast.

Nyong Nyong, Nyongol and Pougug stood at attention by the door. Their soldier-like formation would have tipped us off that something was in the air had it not been conspicuous at first glance. Their lips were bright red, their eyebrows heavily pencilled and their faces dusted over with yellow powder.

'This is Nyong Nyong's doing,' I told Bob. 'It's just like him. Now he's got the others into the cast of his daily drama. Please don't scold — we don't want to hurt their feelings.'

I turned to the self-conscious trio and examined their faces. 'Very clever, Nyong Nyong,' I said. 'Now you'll have to teach the jongoses to dance.'

The laughter they had been suppressing spilled over. I knew the vogue would not last long. After four days of makeup, the novelty was gone and they had to think of some other games to relieve the monotony of routine. We were running a boys' boarding school as well as a hotel, which became clearer when they began staying up half the night gambling, no matter how tired they were the next day.

Two cars had just driven in, but Bob's shrill whistle had brought no response from the kitchen.

'So sorry,' I said, running up. 'All the boys must be in swimming, judging by the shouting from the beach. I'll look for a gardener to carry your baggage.'

Things were getting out of control. What with the boys playing noisy football during afternoon rest hours and all of them going out to swim at tea-time so that there was no one to serve or help with baggage — I realised I would have to learn the rudiments of enforcing discipline.

I found the gardener asleep in his storeroom and shook him. Rubbing his bleary eyes, he ran to the car in his earth-smeared sarong. Not exactly a smooth reception for our guests. I showed the guests to their rooms, and then hurried to the beach.

'Jongos, come quickly,' I called through the roar of the breakers. Nyongol, always quick to learn, was catching a wave with a ten-foot, Honolulu-style board Bob had made. Pougug, with a seven-foot board, was climbing over a swell about to break. But he mistimed and was buried beneath the breaker.

'Nyong Nyong, dress quickly,' I shouted, as annoyed at myself as at him. I always felt I was at fault when anything went wrong. 'Fix cottage Number One. Four guests have just arrived. They'll be angry because no one is there to help them. Tell Nyongol to take Number Four.'

'Tampa, make tea. Trays for four people.'

'Rankop, four extra for dinner. You'll have to kill more chickens. Send the dishwasher to Kuta for vegetables.'

That night after dinner we had a meeting in the kitchen. Bob and I found the boys sitting in a circle on the floor, eyes bright with anticipation of any shared experience — even a scolding. Meetings for correction, suggestions from the servants and pep talks were stimulating and were sometimes suggested by the boys themselves. Bob and I seldom laid down new rules without discussing them in council first. All of us admitted we were inexperienced, so any new policy was considered a trial.

'Tuan and I have been thinking,' I said to open the solemn conference. 'We believe only half of you should swim at one time. What happened today must never happen again. Two people must always be on duty, and more at tea-time. You have not arranged this because no one is in charge in the kitchen. I have no time to watch you. I have to talk to the guests, go sightseeing with them, swim with them, shop with them. I have to sew for the hotel and

do errands in Denpasar. You know I have no time for my painting.
Tuan is always busy too. You know what he has to do. What do
you think we should do?'

'We'll arrange to do better in future,' Rankop said.

'You've said that before,' Bob answered. 'We must have a mandur
(overseer). We know it is not the custom in Bali. Everyone is
equal. No one dares order anyone else. Do you want me to get a
Dutch or Javanese mandur?'

'No . . ,' everyone murmured. They did not want an outsider

invading their private club.

'We don't want a mandur from outside either,' Bob said. 'We want you to have fun but you must remember the guests. If the hotel fails, you will have no work. The better service we give, the more guests, and the more wages and tips for you. Nyonya and I think Nyoman is clever. He can be mandur if you will accept him.

▲ *Bob rides one of his homemade surfboards. He learned surfing in Hawaii before we arrived in Bali.*

When we have something to say, he can tell you. Nyoman is willing.'

'I'll try, Tuan,' he said, obviously itching for the position. He knew he was outstanding because he was the only one at that stage who had mastered the mixing of cocktails. He could not read but he knew the bottles by sight.

The meeting broke up in a cold atmosphere but the experiment was worth trying.

Nyoman sat on a stool in the kitchen, gossiping and smoking while the others worked. He stood at the door, watching the boys carrying dishes to the dining room, criticising this and that. With the meal in progress, he stood in the dining room, posing majestically and calling on a jongos when anyone wanted anything. The boys resented him and called him Tuan Besar — an important man such as the manager of the Bali Hotel. It did not work, and we would have to think of something better. Nyoman was tactfully demoted.

I watched Made Pinatou, our laundryman, take a sheet he had been soaking in hot, soapy water. Holding one end, he threw the other six feet in the air, whence it rippled back in a fluted pile. Over and over, the white column rose and fell. Then he rubbed and slapped it in syncopated rhythm.

His elaborations were like those of all workers. When carpenters drove in a nail or pounded crushed brick to powder to make mortar, they did so in a variety of beats. When I gave wood panels to carvers to cut out designs I had drawn in pencil, they added veins to leaves and petals to flowers, and fancy headdresses and draperies to shadow play figures. Anything to relieve monotony and to make fun out of work.

When a cottage was given a thorough cleaning, the furniture was carried to the sea and the waves became a froth of floating tables and chairs and brown bodies. The hysterical laughter and shrill shouts could be heard far away. Eventually the furniture was scrubbed with coconut husk and sand. Finally, a mass of glistening Balinese and dripping furniture came tearing up the beach to the lawn, where everything was spread out to dry in the sun. The job could have been done with water from the well, but that would have been much too obvious and boring.

Getting on with the Balinese

In spite of the servants' pranks and moments of irresponsibility, they worked desperately hard when necessary, not only in routine jobs but also in the self-imposed task of caring for us or our guests when we were ill. Eleanor Landon, whose name I have mentioned, was an outstanding case.

'Mrs Landon is very sick,' Dr Roestam said. 'No serious ailment but she's in a very rundown condition. She doesn't want to go to hospital, so someone here must look after her all the time.' I did not blame her for wanting to stay with us, for though the primitive hospital in Denpasar had one room for white people no one there spoke English.

Eleanor, a beautiful, delicate young woman with thick auburn hair and violet eyes, was on her way from New Orleans to join her parents on a plantation in Africa. During the four weeks or so she had been with us, she had employed an easy-going Balinese matron to teach her Malay. Together they cycled, swam and went to every entertainment in the neighbourhood. Learning the language easily, Eleanor was able to draw from our boys intimate details of their lives which they dared not tell me.

When she fell ill, the Balinese woman, the logical person to look after her, became paralysed with fear, crying and sniffling and saying she would not know what to do. Eleanor was vomitting often. I had no time for nursing. As if reading my thoughts, the boys moved in of their own accord. All day without a word from me they alternated at her bedside. At night two of them stayed in the room, one asleep on the floor and the other theoretically awake sitting in an armchair.

Every time I went to her cottage to give her medicine, I would find the transparent invalid lying weakly in layers of sheer pink silk and lace, her long hair combed out on the pillow, her milky skin contrasting with the brown figure bending over her, squatting on the floor or tidying up the room. In the morning I would find a boy handing her a wash cloth from a basin of warm water, after he had already bathed her face, arms and feet. During a violent spell, I found Nyong Nyong holding her head over a basin while Rankop balanced her body on a chamber pot on the bed. When she was well enough to be moved, boys carried her to and from the porch several times a day.

One day I found Nyong Nyong sitting beside her, leaning over, dismal with sorrow, for once caught without his prima donna's mantle.

'I fear Nyonya will die,' he said with tears in his eyes. 'She is so good. How can I help her?'

'You're doing all you can,' I said. 'The doctor won't let her die.'

He left to fetch broth from the kitchen, and Eleanor opened her eyes and said, laughing weakly, 'I told Nyong Nyong I was worried about money because my parents seem to have forgotten to send me more.

'He told me not to worry. "You can marry me," he said. "You will live in my village. You will always have enough to eat."'

After three weeks, Eleanor was able to sit up. Her many nurses lessened their vigilance, although continuing to tend and cherish her as they did their 'lucky' pigeons. Soon she left for Java, on her way to her parents.

The boys did not expect the tips she was unable to give, and appreciated her personal gifts such as a cigarette case, a silver ring, a scarf. They stood around tongue-tied as she thanked them and was helped into a taxi. You cannot tell your lucky pigeon just how you feel about it when it is flying away for ever, especially with other people around.

It was a month before Nyong Nyong danced again. He would not admit to a reason, and just said he did not feel well.

Freddie and Arthur got on with the Balinese in another way —

they were initiated into the religion of the island. They achieved by accident something which could not have happened by deliberate intention. Like Eleanor, they made friends easily but instead of learning Malay they memorised a few Balinese phrases. These, with their antics, made them welcome in any village.

Arthur was an artist who was staying with us. Freddie was travelling around the world as companion to a young man from a wealthy family, but while with us he was off duty, as it were. They rode bicycles around together, and would stop wherever Balinese were gathered.

Then Freddie's slapstick clowning would soon have them in stitches. If he saw coolies carrying a pig in a basket strung on a pole, he had to take one end for a few yards. He helped the women carry their loads and clean rice. They were delighted at his clumsy efforts to drop the pounding stick into the hollowed log and catch it on the rebound in rhythm with the others. Not even children were afraid of him, though they had been taught to avoid strangers of any colour — one never knew when an evil spirit might enter an immature soul to cause illness or death.

The breakthrough came at a roadside barong dance in Kuta for a Chinese birthday party. I went with Freddie and Arthur as it is one of the most important and interesting religious performances. The dance represents the conflict between lesser and greater evils. It propitiates Rangda, Bali's most dreaded witch, a horrible monster with a demon's mask, a body covered with long white hair, pendulous breasts and fingernails five inches long.

The Barong is also a terrifying sight but is welcomed as a satanic spirit who tries to keep Rangda under control. He is a long dragon covered with long white or black hair or feathers, formed by a man inside in front and another behind. His snapping jaws and humorous capers enthrall the most apathetic audience. A huge and handsome crown of gilded leather rises between his shoulder blades. His tail stands upright, then droops at the end under the weight of a small mirror and bells. He is full of tricks, threatening one minute and whimsical the next.

When the two confront each other, the Barong makes no sound apart from the tinkling of bells, the clatter of bits of glass and the sharp snapping of his jaws. Rangda roars and bellows horrible curses, bullying and threatening and bursting into obscene laugh-

The kecak dance performances we watched at Bona were described as 'modern' but they seemed primeval. Scores of men wearing only loin cloths took part, their bodies gleaming in the lamplight. They chanted and hissed, and burst into vigorous, turbulent movements marked by extended, trembling arms and fingers. A lone figure in their midst pulled himself up until he seemed eight feet tall. The kecak was always popular with tourists, and with us, no matter how many times we watched. More pictures on following pages.

ter, rocking back on her heels, long nails quivering. Together they enact their way through all manner of stories.

At the end of the performance, fifteen men or more rush on to the stage, already in a self-induced trance Stripped to loin cloths, they flourish krisses, taut and trembling, shouting like madmen. They attack Rangda but she waves them off. Eventually Rangda works them into such a state that they turn their krisses upon themselves. With screeches and shouts, their arm muscles tense and locked, sometimes rolling on the ground, they strive to drive the krisses into their chests.

Rarely does a kris penetrate the skin. We heard of only one serious result. A man in a trance stabbed Rangda through the heart.

Men appointed as guards disarm each dancer, one holding him by the hair, the other twisting the kris out of his convulsed fist. A priest or priestess holds a bowl of smoking charcoal and leaves to each dancer's face and another sprinkles him with holy water. If he does not come to his senses, he is led to the

Barong and his face wiped with its holy beard of human hair. Then he is laid on a mat to rest. Frequently men lie still tense, pounding their chests, groaning and weeping.

Three of the trance dancers I saw with Freddie and Arthur refused to respond to treatment. I left, tired from standing by the roadside, breathing in dust and being pushed by the excited crowd.

'What a night!' Freddie said late next morning.

'What a night!' echoed Arthur.

'Tell me the truth,' I said. 'What were you doing all night?'

'We went on an expedition with the Barong,' Freddie said. 'Those kris boys had really knocked themselves out. Some of the guards half carried them up the road on the run and everyone followed, even the musicians with their instruments. We went with the crowd, shouting like everyone else.'

'Where did you go?'

'To a temple, I don't know where. We ran for miles.'

'Come on — tell the rest.'

'We all went into the temple courtyard, where an important looking priest worked over the men, and brought them around after a while. Everyone was having a great time. We kidded with them, using all the Balinese words we had. They seemed to like us. Things got to the point where they were talking about initiating us into their religion.

'Half the crowd tried to put us out while the other half tried to keep us in. They really went for each other, until the ones who wanted us out gave in. Then they snatched off our shirts and tried to take off our shoes. We couldn't see ourselves walking home barefoot, so we managed to keep them.'

Freddie and Arthur had gone to the show in sarongs and head-cloths. Naturally, the crowd wanted to remove their European accessories.

'They made us kneel in front of an altar,' Freddie continued, 'and taught us how to say our prayers in Balinese, holding flowers in our fingers and throwing them to the ground. They did a

◄ *Rangda, Bali's most dreaded witch, roars and bellows horrible curses.*

ceremony over us and gave us new names.'

'So, what do we call you?'

'I'm Made Rai and Arthur is Putu Gede.'

This parody of religion was similar to others I had seen incorporated into barong plays. It was not considered disrespectful. News of the frolic spread from Kuta to Denpasar the same day. After that no one seeing Freddie and Arthur cycling to town in their headcloths failed to call them by their new names. We did too. We never called them anything but Made and Putu.

Being democratic with the Balinese could sometimes backfire, however. One of our guests, Major Martyr, an Englishman, was on holiday from Japan where he had lived for thirty years and taught English to members of the royal family. He was a great mixer who liked to go around in shorts, a short Japanese jacket open at the front and bare feet. He was popular with the boys, who especially admired a jewelled sword presented to him by the Emperor of Japan. It was a kris more handsome than any they had ever seen. Every day the room boy laid it respectfully on the major's bed as if placing it on an altar for worship.

One day Major Martyr told me one of the boys had just scolded him for a serious mistake the previous evening. He had disgraced the hotel by sitting on the ground drinking arak with coolies.

'Your boy cried real tears when he lectured me,' he said. 'He told me I had lost caste and must never do such a thing again.'

The incident began when the major went to the boy's village for a celebration. He was with a European woman who had lived in Bali for several years, whom I shall call Mrs Wattle. I asked the boy what had happened.

'I was so ashamed,' he said fiercely. 'Nyonya Wattle told Tuan Major he could sit on the ground. Then she made jokes about him in Balinese to the people of my village. Everyone was laughing at him.'

'Couldn't you stop it?'

'I couldn't do anything against Nyonya Wattle. My people laughed when she made jokes about his jacket, his bare feet, about an important person acting like a coolie. I had to tell him. I hope you are not angry.'

I was not angry because he was right.

Leekas

About a year from the day we moved to Kuta, a child-sized Balinese with large, soulful eyes appeared at our kitchen door. We did not know it at the time, but he was to save us from complete exhaustion. He turned out to be a mastermind among the other boys and, more important, he had the highest standards of honour and honesty. He was Wayan Leekas, a name I record here with reverence.

Speaking in good Malay and with hands correctly clasped, he said he was working for a white woman who shared her cottage and bath-house with one of her servants. She even allowed him to sit at the dining table with her — and he a man of no caste. If a Balinese high caste woman were caught in such a relationship, she would cease to exist for the people of her village. Before the Dutch occupation, both offenders would have been thrown in the sea.

Leekas said his employer had periodic quarrels with her servant, during which they both cried hysterically and the man would pack his clothes and go home 'until death'. After a few days the woman would go in her car and pick him up for another round. The last row had ended with the servant striking her cheek so hard that she was too bruised to appear in public for a week. We knew this story was true.

'I had a frank talk with her,' Leekas said. 'I told her that if she allowed her servant to come back I would leave immediately. She swore she would never allow him in her house again. She begged me to stay. She said she would make me her chauffeur and raise my wages, and give me her house if she left Bali. All empty words. If the servant comes back, can I work here?'

About three weeks later Leekas wrote to say his employer was back with her servant, and he 'could not stand any more comedy'. He came to us apparently frightened and submissive but — we were to find later — with steel in his spine.

For the first few days he came to announce meals by kneeling some distance from us, with hands folded as if in prayer and his big, brown eyes deep with sadness. There he waited until someone noticed him, when he would say in a small voice, 'Pardon me, you may eat now.'

At first he was just one of the boys but he soon attracted our special notice because he never got confused and even sought responsibility. In a pinch, he would take the initiative. He could drive a car and knew all the roads in Bali. His experience as an organiser for dance and drama companies had taught him much about entertainments. He could be sent alone to Denpasar in the car to carry out the most complicated errands. He gladly sacrificed his time off if we needed him.

Leekas' young and pretty wife, Lesug, had been trained in the peculiar singing and mannerisms of the drama and in the high Balinese and Kawi languages used by high caste characters. Her

▲ *Leekas and, right, Lesug, his wife. He was a mastermind who helped us run the hotel while she was a talented classical actress and singer. Their marriage seemed to me the only romantic one I heard of among the Balinese. — Picture of Lesug by courtesy of their son, Made Adi Susila.*

manners and smooth, graceful movements made me feel like a bull in a china shop. Because of her poised and beautifully proportioned figure, she got eightyfive cents of a guilder an hour for posing for artists while the standard rate was fifty cents.

Leekas built a three-roomed house on a back corner of our lot, and at times it would be like a salon with Leekas and Lesug receiving relatives and friends. Sometimes there would be twenty or thirty visitors. Visiting chauffeurs slept in the extra room. When I went to visit, Lesug would treat me like a queen and insist that her frightened baby do likewise.

We were approaching the end of our physical endurance.

'You have become a good jongos in a few weeks,' Bob told Leekas. 'Others take months to learn. You know we need a mandur. Nothing goes well because we have no time to watch everything. Would you like to take charge?'

'It is not customary,' Leekas said, his eyes wide with disapproval. 'The jongoses would not accept me.'

'If you will not try, we'll have to get a Dutch man' — the most potent threat we could invent.

Leekas' normally worried expression turned to alarm. I could see he was engaged in a conflict between ambition and discretion.

'Try to understand, Leekas,' I said. 'We are very tired. We are not used to the heat and malaria. We are getting more guests, and we must spend time with them so they will like the hotel. Now we have twentyfive people working for us, and more working part-

▲ *Even working women possessed a proud dignity.*

170

time. Please try to help us.'

The word 'help' has a special meaning in Bali. To serve as a domestic, to offer hospitality, to give presents is to help. If anyone helps you, you must give in return in whatever way you can. We gave clothes to our boys, rented their bicycles to guests for them, lent them money, took care of them when they were sick and helped their families. In return they invited us to their family and village ceremonies, and brought us duck, pork or turtle meat from their feasts.

The appeal was too much for Leekas. With an expression of concentrated worry, he agreed to start at once. He was to be in charge of the jongoses, gardeners and extra workers but must leave the temperamental Rankop entirely alone. There was dynamite in that kitchen.

For the first few days he behaved as if nothing had changed. He felt his way so that his authority crept up on the boys without their feeling it. At times I had to tell him to bear down hard, as when boys spent an hour or more in the Kuta market gossiping or flirting. They resented being regimented, and there was rebellion in the air. Then Leekas would say, 'If anyone thinks he can do my job, I'll change with him.' He meant it but no one volunteered.

Eventually he made out the bills, accompanied guests as a guide, brought news of entertainments, arranged dances, made charts of the rooms showing who was where and who was expected, paid bills and wages, kept track of chits, drove our car when necessary, engaged models for photographers, and took charge of the dining room. With all three of us doing our best, we evolved a life that was not only bearable but fun. I even had time to paint.

Leekas was upset one day because he felt that he talked too much about his hard childhood while taking guests around the villages. As a result the tourists felt sorry for him and gave him tips. He thought this not right. I told him they gave tips because they liked him and because he helped them. But he decided he should practise some restraint.

'Never again will I tell anyone how my grandfather sold our ricefields for opium,' he said. 'Or about the times when I had no money and no rice to eat. I often cried from hunger.'

'If you had been rich,' I said, 'your raja (not a real one, but the relative governing his district) would not have treated you like a son. He would not have sent you to school or taught you high caste manners. Now you write like us and like your own people as well.'

'True,' Leekas said with a touch of pride, 'Also, I might have thrown my money away on cockfights instead of becoming a dancer.'

Proof that Leekas was a success as mandur came after he had had a spell in hospital, critically ill with malaria, pneumonia and asthma. One of our guests gave us a bottle of a new sulfa drug, we gave it to the doctor, and the doctor — though his dignity would not permit him to admit it — must have used it, because Leekas' recovery was miraculous. Now he was back home, his convalescence a constant misery to me because he worried about not being on the job.

But he was. The servants often visited him to ask his advice on many matters. They needed his help particularly in dividing the tips. The boys had decided to pool all in a bamboo 'bank' nailed to the kitchen wall. When the bank was split open with a knife at the end of each month, everyone shared. Leekas and Bob were the judges as to how much each deserved. The more the responsibility, the greater the share. Behind closed doors, they counted and stacked and figured like money-lenders.

Until Leekas was strong enough to walk, I went to his house each morning, and Lesug and I would carry him to an outdoor couch with a thick mattress and clean sheets, where he could watch the chickens scratching in the dust and the swayback pig ploughing up the yard.

Next to fall ill was Leekas' and Lesug's baby. At seven months, it showed symptoms of worms. I had tutored them carefully but somehow the rules had been broken. While Leekas and Lesug observed good hygiene in feeding the baby, they could not control the old women who ran the show the moment their back was turned. These were the sort of people who would use filthy fingers to thrust chewed gobs of rice and banana into a baby's mouth.

Dr Roestam looked at the baby and left worm medicine which was to be followed in two days by castor oil. When it came to getting the oil into a very strong baby, Lesug was as inexperienced as I was. She held him while I forced the spoon into his mouth and then held his nose to make him swallow, but he would not. He would choke to death first. He bellowed and strangled until his face was blue. Half a pint of castor oil was smeared all over him, all over my dress and hands and all over Lesug's naked body from chin to waist.

Just as we were giving up, Leekas rode in on his bicycle. He held the baby and put the last spoonful of oil into its mouth. It went down as easily as syrup.

'Tell me how you married Lesug,' I said.

In the afternoons, when we had time, Leekas taught me Balinese while I taught him English. This was such a time.

'I met Lesug when we were both playing in an ardja (a light opera). We wanted to marry but we had no money. She comes from a rich family but I had nothing. We had to work for two years to save enough for a home and a wedding ceremony. We acted and danced together. We spent nothing on pleasure.'

'What did you have to pay Lesug's family?'

'They would not take a cent from me because our families were friends. This causes me much trouble because I am always indebted to them. Whenever they want me to help in the ricefields I must go. If they give a party, I must help entertain. I wish I could pay them and be free.'

Lesug's family had been clever to insist on such a bargain. They could not have had a more talented and conscientious son-in-law.

'What about Lesug's acting? I don't see her leaving on her bicycle any more.'

'I don't let her. She was called so often that people were quarrelling over her. That makes trouble. She is twentytwo now, an old woman. It is not becoming for her to act.'

I could not convince Leekas that she was a pretty girl in the bloom of youth, though he admitted she was still good to look at.

Leekas' marriage to Lesug seemed to me the only romantic one I heard of among the Balinese, but Leekas could not appreciate my point as the Balinese have no word for it.

We talked about dancing. Leekas said that when he was small he danced in a janger, a social, seated dance by twelve boys and twelve girls. 'I was a good dancer. I liked it. I wanted to make a janger myself when I left school. I trained the boys and girls until they were good enough to show to anyone.'

'Where did you get money for costumes?'

'I borrowed it from my raja. We had the best crowns for the girls and the best collars for the boys. Rangda's costume alone cost fiftyfive guilders. I told the raja I was going to take my janger to Java to make money and pay him back. He said, "You may not go. You will get lost."'

To even suggest such a trip was daring for a lad so young. He later organised a janger for us — the best I have ever seen.

'Then you became an actor?'

'I did. I studied with an old man who gave me lessons free. Then I became a head man. Lesug was one of my actresses. She had studied in a school for drama. She could sing high Balinese in a beautiful voice. Her acting was correct according to the old traditions. That's why people still seek her.'

'Are you sorry that you can't act now?'

'No, I have to eat. That always comes first. I make much more money as your jongos. In the ardja I made only three or four guilders a night. We played only four or five times a month. When I have saved three hundred guilders I shall buy a rice field. I shall never be hungry again. My son will never be hungry.'

He did buy his ricefield, and he was on his way to buying another when we left Bali.

We talked about the war then going on between China and Japan. I asked how Bali would fare if the war spread and Bali were cut off from other countries.

'I've already thought about this,' he said. 'We have everything we need. If we have no bicycles and cars, we can walk as we used to. We do not need shirts and coats. We grow some cotton and could grow more to make sarongs. There is plenty of food for everyone. Every year we send away rice, pigs and cows. If we keep all for ourselves, we'll have more than we need.'

He was so right, but he had not allowed that war could also mean Bali falling under the thumb of a rapacious occupier who would take most of everything for himself.

Training servants

On slack afternoons I hit the kulkul, the hollowed log tomtom, hanging beside the kitchen and called out, 'School! School! Everyone! Don't forget paper and pencils.'

When we began the hotel I had to run, rain or shine, from kitchen to cottages, answering the guests' kulkuls. Later, if a jongos went, he took a writing pad for written requests — but I had to be on hand to read and translate them. Rudimentary English was so necessary that I found the more ambitious boys huddled in pairs, at any time of the day, with lists of words and Malay-English dictionaries.

My students were always excited at sitting around a table with me because they felt their place was on the floor. But eyelids drooped after thirty minutes of 'How do you do, Sir . . . Your room is ready, Madam . . . Would you like tea?' Yet the novelty of sitting on chairs, and remaining seated even if guests happened to walk through, and doing something important in a group, made the effort bearable.

Rankop and Leekas were the only ones who came to the hotel knowing how to write, but some of the others, over the months and years, made good progress. But not everyone was pleased with our effort.

'Surely you don't let the jongoses speak English?' a Dutch guest from Java said grimly. 'We don't allow our Javanese servants to use anything except Malay. We don't want them to know what we are saying in Dutch.'

'Indeed, I do let them,' I said with feeling. 'I do my best to persuade them to speak English. You forget that for every guest we have from the Dutch Indies we have ten from other parts of the world.'

'Ah, so,' he answered sceptically. 'Perhaps it is different here.'

Indeed it was different. Courses in English, housework and bartending were only a beginning. We also had to teach western manners and customs.

One of the most difficult to teach was the need to knock before entering a room. There is little privacy in the Balinese way of life. Changing clothes in an open pavilion is only a matter of slipping a different sarong over the original which is then dropped from underneath. Our habit of lying in bed in the nude is unheard of.

Our boys at first took it for granted that bedrooms were semi-public places. Several guests complained that boys entered when they were undressed, silent as cats in their bare feet. They had not withdrawn when they saw the guests were unclothed but had gone about their business as if they were alone — which they were, in their way of thinking. I taught the boys how to knock on doors, but they would slip occasionally from lifelong habit.

Throughout, we found that the best incentive to learning and good service was an appeal to pride in the hotel, because the Balinese are jealous and competitive. They gloried in Bob's little victories when he won at tennis or came home with an ashtray for winning an obstacle race with his car. No rebuke was more effective than, 'The hotel will have a bad name if jongoses make mistakes like the one you made yesterday'.

That particular mistake involved a novel interpretation of an instruction to change sheets. The jongos, a new one, told me he had tried to follow my thoughts, and had turned the sheets over so the 'clean' sides faced each other.

The old gardeners required a technique of their own. One, the fifth in a long line, arrived for initiation. His first duty in the morning was to clean the bath and toilet. He had never seen such a contraption before. I demonstrated with broom, pail, disinfectant, cleaner, brush and cloth, polishing everything, talking in Malay with each move. I asked once in a while if he understood, and when he grunted assumed he did.

I asked him to repeat the cleaning process. In a few broken words, half Malay, half low Balinese, he said he had not understood me. The corners of his mouth twitched and tears rolled down his wrinkled cheeks. He started crying so hard I took him to the kitchen and asked Rankop to find out what was wrong. The old man did not know Malay and was afraid, I was told.

Bob took over. Although he had a smaller vocabulary than me, he was patient and used the fewest words possible. He made himself understood while I went into whys and wherefors. So the old man was freed from my clutches, though he continued to burst into tears at the sight of me.

After months of work training a new boy, we might lose him and have to start from scratch with another. A storm at night during our third rainy season triggered such a departure. The wind was furious, the studio rocked — and rain streamed in. I looked up to see lightning through a long slit in the roof where the thatch had been blown up on end. Bob and I flew into action moving everything which would be damaged by water to the dry side of the room.

'Oh, Lord,' I moaned 'Think of the cottages. Suppose this happens to all of them. How can we face our guests in the morning?'

Early in the morning, picturing furious guests leaving in a body, I went to the dining room. It was a lake. All the windows were open, one had been broken by a falling tile, and Potier, the jongos who was supposed to close all the front windows in a storm, was fast asleep on a bench. He had slept even through the crashing of the glass window.

'Get up, Potier,' I said, shaking him. 'What kind of a watchman are you? Go at once for the Chinese tailor in Kuta. We must take off all the covers and they must be washed before mould starts. We must air the cushions in the sun so they won't smell.'

Potier was too dumbfounded to answer. We had had great hopes for him at first because he could read and write, but he was a gloomy person. His perpetual depression was due to a woman who would have none of him. She tossed off his shy advances with ribald laughter and shrill teasing from behind her vegetable stand in the Kuta market. As a result Potier moved in a fog.

Feeling ill with worry, I went to the cottages and found the

windows of all the porches wide open, mattresses and cushions soaked through. The thatched roofs were intact, however, so we did not have to fear an outraged exodus, but things were bad enough. All day we rushed soggy mounds of cushions in and out between showers. After the covers had been washed and dried, the tailor, the boys' wives and I sewed them on again. Our laundryman washed and dried like a fiend, his brass flatirons scorching hot, his bare stomach covered with a bathmat to prevent burning.

Beside myself with haste and annoyance, I drove everyone all day, taking a dig at Potier every time I saw him. Although Bob and I felt sorry for him, we decided we dare not risk another such upset. We took him to the office to discharge him.

'I heard the window break,' he said, 'but I couldn't wake up. I'm

↟ *Dinner in the garden at the Kuta Beach Hotel, with everyone smiling for the camera and the boy on the left enjoying a joke of his own.*

so heartsick over that woman that I can't sleep or I sleep too much. Let me try again. I'll do better.'

'We're very sorry,' Bob said quietly. 'We must let you go. After you are married, come back to us.'

Later on, having lost his fancy to a sturdier man, Potier found a job at the Bali Hotel, where the work was more specialised and less demanding.

Another boy, Pougig, presented us with a brief but memorable experience. He was a homely, lanky man of thirty with no experience but a will to learn. But no sooner had we taught him to be a help rather than a hindrance than he developed marital complications. As he was a widower and making more money than ever before, he hastened to remarry.

He picked out a widow in Legian. After the ceremony, both her father and her deceased husband's father demanded payment for her. The local court decided in favour of her father — but Pougig had not been with us long enough to save any money, and his new wife was penniless.

'I ask for permission to go to the police station,' he said unexpectedly one day.

'What for?'

'A small matter.'

'What have you done?'

'I cannot pay for my wife.'

'When you married you knew you would have to pay for her. Why didn't you wait until you'd saved enough?'

'Because I was afraid someone else would get her.'

'How much do you have to pay?'

'Forty guilders.'

'What will the police do?'

'They will put us both in jail for three weeks.'

'Aren't you ashamed to go to jail?'

'No, Nyonya. It is soon over. When we get out, we owe nothing. I need pay only the price of the ceremony.'

So Pougig and his wife went to jail. We did not try to help them as Pougig's act had been irresponsible and he had not been with us long enough for us to feel any obligation.

A week later, driving through the main street of Denpasar, I saw a dozen prisoners in khaki uniforms, carrying brooms and shovels. Someone called, and I saw Pougig waving and pointing laughingly at his trousers. He knew I disagreed with the Balinese wearing trousers instead of sarongs. I asked him how he liked prison. 'It's all right, Nyonya,' he said, 'except that there's no spice in the food.'

Dishwashing in the Indies is painful to watch in most households, and the sensitive housewife does well to stay away from the kitchen after meals. In Java and Bali it takes place entirely on the floor, except in a few houses where a strict mistress has won.

Our boys always stripped for action, tying up sarongs and squatting on their heels. Pans of hot water in different stages of soapiness, tottering mounds of dirty dishes, cans of garbage — some for the chickens, some for burning or burying — covered every available space.

As the washers slopped the dishes from one pan to another, dirty water spilled in rivulets and flooded the whole porch. The breakage rate on the bare cement was appalling. Later in the day the jongoses gathered to dry and polish. Though inefficient and time wasting, the method created a social occasion not easily

▲ No shirt, but as much dignity as if he were wearing full formal dress. Of course I enjoyed meeting and painting such people.

abandoned.

Bob and I decided to change things. One day after lunch we asked for two large pans of water with hot water in reserve, soap and clean towels. We would show the boys a better way. The whole staff watched as Bob washed and I dried.

But soon the audience grew restless with this reversal of roles, and tried to take the dishes out of our hands. We had said we would wash and dry twelve people's dishes in fortyfive minutes. When we finished within forty, they clapped as they had seen tourists do at dances. (If the Balinese like a performance, they show it by staying to the end; if they do not like it, they walk away.)

'Now you see how to do it,' Bob said. 'Look at the silver and glasses — how bright they are. Starting tonight, try to do the same.'

The next day we found the usual litter on the floor, and the usual swill of suds and bits of garbage. Our system was never attempted. Leisurely hours sitting were better than nervous minutes standing.

Like all other employers in the Orient, we expected so much of our servants at the low standard wages that I was embarrassed when our boys encountered service along western lines. They happened to see a top bracket case.

A very large and very new car swept up the drive. From the rear emerged a white man in a dark suit, carrying an armful of men's clothes on hangers. He addressed Bob with deference, asking where he might find the room which Lord and Lady Beatty had reserved the previous day.

'Yes, of course, they're to be in Number Seven, right over there,' Bob replied.

I was in the kitchen thinking about lunch. The boys, who always watched new arrivals with intense interest, asked who the new tuan was, and why he was carrying his clothes in his arms.

'He's the jongos of the tuan and nyonya who came here yesterday to book a cottage.'

Their mouths fell open. That a well-dressed white man could be a jongos passed understanding.

'How much is he paid?' I was ashamed to mention a monthly

wage several times what they earned in half a year.

'What does he do?'

'He takes care of the tuan's clothes, packs the suitcases, buys tickets and cigarettes, polishes shoes, and, well, perhaps he knows how to drive a car too.'

'What does he eat? Where does he eat?'

'Oh, he eats the same food as the tuan and nyonya. In the Bali Hotel he eats in the dining room with the other guests, but he has a table to himself.'

This was really too much for them to take in all at once. A silence followed while the facts were digested.

Lord and Lady Beatty arrived in the same impressive car — and with another white woman sitting in the back with them. She stepped out first, her arms full of dresses, and walked straight to the cottage while the other two strolled to the beach. While she put the clothes away I talked to her. She was a quietly dressed, middle-aged woman preoccupied with her lady's comfort.

In the kitchen the boys were in a huddle.

'Who is the other guest? There are only two beds in Number Seven. Should we make up a bed on the porch?'

'No, the extra nyonya is the babu (maid) of the other nyonya.'

'How much is a babu paid? What does a babu do?'. . . And away we went again, with me trying to think what she might do in addition to sewing and pressing.

When our guests were settled into their cottage, the maid left, returning to the Bali Hotel where she and the valet, her husband, occupied the suite abandoned by their employers for our humble cottage.

Lord and Lady Beatty were like runaway children, laughing at the fun of turning their luxurious room over to their servants while they felt they had the better of the bargain.

Fortunately, the high wages and easy services of the maid and valet were consigned to the realm of freak phenomena characteristic of the unknown regions inhabited by white people. No comparisons were drawn which might invite resentment. No revolution occurred. After the departure of Tuan Jongos and Nyonya Babu, our boys carried on peacefully, giving their best efforts to creating comfort and glamour for others and living meagrely on the fringes of our relative opulence.

A new car, a new water system

During our second year Bob found that the hotel had earned the price of a new car. As we needed kitchen equipment, I was the one elected to go to Java for it.

Three Javanese in pyjama pants hoisted the triangular sail of their prau and we sailed out of Gilimanuk into the swift currents of the straits between Bali and Java. We heeled over, shipping whitecaps. Our old jalopy nearly filled the boat. Rankop huddled in the back seat, so terrified that he fell asleep to avoid the sight of approaching disaster. Two of our guests at the hotel were helping me wrestle the nearly defunct car to Surabaya. Charlie Brower, who was travelling to cure himself of drinking, and his friend Jim Connally would leave us there, and Rankop would help with the driving back to Bali.

On the Java side, a hand winch pulled us up a heavy log ramp to solid ground just as the clouds burst over our heads. Rain poured through the broken curtains and around the ill-fitting windshield, soaking us in a few minutes. The engine stopped every few feet. The starter refused to work so the men had to labour with the crank, which seemed set in solid rubber. We searched the back streets of Banjuwangi for a garage where three mechanics spent an hour and a half fixing things.

The rain stopped as the first tyre exploded and we slid across the road. Three miles further on, another blow-out, and we laboured to fit on our last spare. The jack worked only for a few inches, so we had to use rocks and logs as well. The job took more than an hour and all three men were covered in mud. We were so tired and exasperated that we laughed with tears in our eyes.

As darkness fell the rain returned, one headlight went out and the windscreen wiper stopped. Streams of water on the glass turned oncoming cars into a blaze of light. Driving became insanity and we looked for an inn for the night.

That was a bad day. The next day was better — we got to Surabaya, I bought a new Chevrolet for a staggering price, and I went shopping also for pots, dishes, glasses, books, socks and presents for the boys. The third day was back to being bad news as I rocked in bed, violently ill from smoked fish I had eaten in our big, modern hotel the previous day. The retching lasted all day. Rankop sat on the floor, holding a basin in one hand and my head in the other. That night he slept on the verandah tiles outside my door.

Two days later we loaded our shiny car, added a box of eight fat pigeons for Bob, and headed back towards Bali. The road which had nearly shaken our teeth out when we travelled by jalopy was now as smooth as glass. And so were the straits for the crossing to Bali. We swept up the coral drive of the Kuta Beach Hotel blowing the horn triumphantly.

This was a high spot of our Bali adventure so far — the hotel had earned a gleaming new car (or, rather, it would have done when the last payment was made). Bob took all the boys for a ride, five or six at a time. It was exhilarating, a counterpoint to the perpetual state of crisis in which we lived and which we complained about often — though actually we loved it.

Bob attached a three-note French horn to the battery, indulged in shameless exhibitionism for two weeks, and one day came home with new licence plates.

'They take the place of the temporary ones from Java,' he explained.

The number on the plates was 100. I asked Bob how he had got such a special number, and he replied that he had just asked for it.

But there was something wrong. Our Dutch friends snickered when examining the car. It was not the usual way of showing admiration. Finally I asked why.

'It's the number,' I was told. '100 is the sign we use on our public toilets.' I learned that the English also talk about going to 'the loo'.

But Bob liked it, so it remained.

Weeks passed but the car remained a novelty, as important to the boys as it was to us. Not only did it raise the hotel's prestige in their eyes, but it also could be borrowed to help celebrate a birthday, a wedding or the anniversary of some nearby gamelan.

'Nyonya, good news!' Leekas said breathlessly. 'A procession in Denpasar this afternoon for Queen Wilhelmina's birthday. A competition. May we borrow the car? We'll decorate it.'

'You mean you might win a prize?'

'Maybe. But we just heard. Others have had two days to prepare. We can't do as well — but we want to try.'

'Go ahead,' I said. 'But I don't know who will look after the hotel while the workers play.'

'Don't worry,' he said eagerly. 'I'll send for men from Legian.' He could get a gang of volunteers for the asking for an adventure of this kind.

The boys already had experience decorating the car, festooning it with green branches, flowers, coloured paper streamers and strings of paper flags. Dressed in their brightest clothes and waving Dutch and American flags, banging drums and dishpans and shouting wildly, they would drive slowly up and down the streets of Kuta to impress the neighbours. Then they would head for some village celebration, returning later so noisily that we could hear them blocks away, like some jungle rite.

On this occasion, as Leekas had predicted, a crowd of workers assembled at the garage. Bapak ('Father') Runtung, our now full-time carpenter who fixed things when windows dropped off rusty hinges, pressure lamps would not work or termites undermined the foundations of a house, was called in to help.

He built a frame of wood and bamboo which gradually covered the whole car. When it was sheathed in paper, it took the form of a giant fish with headlights for eyes and a forked tail curving from the trunk rack. All hands cut multi-coloured scales from coloured paper and glued them on. Gaping jaws with rows of white fangs projected from the radiator. Fishing nets and baskets were draped along the running boards. There never had been such a Chevrolet before.

The lucky men who would ride in the car, chosen by some tacit agreement, borrowed white fishermen's clothes. The finishing touch, which only Balinese would consider related to the project, was added by three men from Legian who whipped up monkey costumes of black hair from palm trees with carved masks and long tails. The total effect (though a little confused) was sensational. Twenty people had completed the job in a few hours with concentration not always conspicuous in the daily work of the hotel.

▲ Bob and a glimpse of our car, almost hidden in the garage. Our water tank is concealed within this building, which we judged the most artistic we had.

As the car drove off, the fishermen inside beat drums and the monkeys clung to the running boards. Kuta was treated to a thorough preview of what Denpasar had yet to see. The boys' effort did not win a prize, but they all had such fun that any award would have been irrelevant.

A year or so later the big problem was water. 'We can't wait any longer,' Bob exclaimed one day with a finality which left no room for my fears of bankruptcy.

'Don't tell me you're going to start on that water tower?' I said. 'Didn't you estimate the cost of the frame alone at $900? How will you pay for it?'

'Don't you see that we're making money now?' Bob said. 'You didn't think we'd be able to pay for the two single cottages or the private baths for each bedroom — but we were.'

'Yes, I know. Everything has turned out as you expected. But there's a war coming in Europe. Suppose you start and everything crashes? The few tourists we get from Java wouldn't keep the place going.'

'Leave that to me,' Bob said, turning towards the office to order materials. He already had plans from an engineer in Denpasar.

We had earlier built a small water tower. When the expensive teak frame was completed, a government engineer said it might supply a dribble of water to the kitchen, but not a drop beyond. So it was converted into a store room, and Bob was as happy as if he had not lost hard earned money — at least something had been achieved.

As Krinting was busy, Bob employed Gusti Oka, our former landlord in Denpasar, a skilled builder. The frame would rise from a base thirty feet square to a tank platform twentytwo feet above the ground. Gusti Oka made four big cement blocks at the corners, and laid out Borneo ironwood supports on the ground with iron girders between, to see how they looked. Problem: How were these supports to be raised into position?

Ingeniously, Gusti Oka built a conical core of long bamboo poles like a giant teepee. An army of men heaved the monstrous ironwood supports upright against the bamboo, the girders were bolted into place and the core was removed. We had a structure which would withstand the strongest gale of the north-west monsoon.

In north Bali, Bob found a cast-off thousand gallon tank, scraped off a thick layer of rust inside and lined it with cement. To raise it to the platform, Gusti Oka built a ramp such as is used at cremations for carrying the body to its resting place in the tower, but higher, broader and sturdier.

With a gang of about twenty men pushing the tank and each other, and with another gang pulling on long ropes, the tank was urged up the ramp amid hearty shouting and bellowed orders until it slid into place at the top. Throughout, Bob ran up and down the ramp like a monkey, blond hair flying and white trousers flapping around his long legs. I stood below, hoping the tank would not slide back and crush the workmen.

The tower was completed with a two-storey, tiered exterior of thatch and stained  bamboo walls to become the most artistic and Oriental building we had. Inside, the space was divided into a four-car garage, a laundry, a dormitory for our boys and an engine room for the secondhand generator which supplied power to Bob's darkroom.

'It's magnificent,' I said. 'Our dining room should look as beautiful. But you haven't done anything about the water.'

'That will come in a few weeks. You'll see. I'm going to have two wells with hand pumps so that even if one is out of order we can use the other.'

This was reassuring. At that time we had hand-filled oil drums outside the bathrooms to keep toilet cisterns filled. If we switched to running water, we would need to be sure the system could not break down.

Bob and Bapak Runtung, the carpenter, made a wood mould, put

Another view of our water tank building, which provided much needed extra space and merged nicely amid the coconut palms.

heavy construction wire inside, poured in concrete — and produced a series of pipes four feet in diameter, five feet high and five inches thick. Four of them, sunk into the ground one above the other, would make a well twenty feet deep.

Men dug what looked like a bomb crater and the first section, weighing four hundred pounds or more, was slid to the bottom amid hoarse cries of warning and alarm, almost as good a show as raising the tank. A man jumped inside to dig out sand and throw out water, and the pipe slowly settled deeper. The outside was packed with sand, and the second pipe was rolled down with the same rumpus and placed neatly on top. The seam between the two was plastered with cement and allowed to dry for two days.

But the pipes, though there was much water inside, were not yet deep enough. Four men with buckets on ropes dipped the water out, racing against more water seeping in. When only a few inches remained, a man jumped in and dug furiously with his hands, filling more buckets with sand. When he was up to his waist in water he was helped out, blue with cold. The two pipes had sunk considerably.

Digging continued the following day, with men who could not stand the cold any longer being hauled out and others taking their place. So it went until all four pipes had been sunk into position and the well was deep enough. A circular, foot-thick matt of black hair from a certain palm tree which will last fifteen years under water was sunk to the bottom of the well and held down by heavy stones as a filter.

A brick parapet was built around the top, a concrete lid was eased into position and a pump was installed. Because men had been working in the water, the well was pumped out for several hours. A government health inspector declared all in order. We started on the second well. . .

When water began to flow to the kitchen and the bathrooms, excitement rose like a fever. Tubs and sinks were continually filled to the brim and jongoses forgot to turn off taps. Weeks passed before the higher strata of our servants could be persuaded to consider the coolies working like galley slaves at the pumps.

To the Balinese, running water seemed too good to be true. But I was even more impressed than them because the water tower, the wells and all the fittings were paid for within six months.

A pair of plagues

A rustling below woke me from a doze. I leaned over the studio balcony in time to see the door to the beach closing slowly. That must be the thief! I ran down in bare feet as a long whistle pierced the air. Someone else had seen him.

Outside the door, a painting and a packet of cigarettes lay on the ground, dropped by the thief in his hurry to escape. Four of our boys dashed across the garden, Sabah in the lead. They ran on to the beach, and moments later returned, Sabah holding a lad of about nine by the arm.

Sabah said the boys, worried by a spate of thefts, had been taking turns to keep watch from the kitchen. They were concerned that one of them would be suspected. Guests left money and jewellery in their rooms and it was important that the boys be above suspicion.

I told Sabah he was a good jongos, and asked, 'Now what do we do about this boy?'

'Call the punggawa,' said several voices, referring to the local magistrate.

The boy appeared indifferent and superior, denying everything. He had never seen the painting before. He had never been in the studio. 'Let me go,' he demanded impudently.

Bob asked how the boy could have so much nerve.

'He's a high caste from Kuta. He doesn't think he'll be punished. But I saw him come out of the studio,' said Sabah.

Leekas left with the car and returned with the punggawa, a middle-aged man with a walrus moustache who moved with solemn dignity. We told him what had happened, what was missing, and he wrote in a small notebook. Leekas took him and the boy back to his office in Kuta — and that was the end of the matter. The punggawa no doubt let the charge languish because he was no higher in caste than the delinquent.

But Sabah had distinguished himself, which was good for his excessive modesty. Leekas' friend, he was a gentle and self-effacing man of thirty with intensely sensitive features. He had over-large eyes with doll-like lashes. When he received his wages he almost prostrated himself with gratitude.

'Do not say thank you,' I would say. 'You are not receiving a present. You work hard and you receive money for your work. You owe nothing.'

'Thank you too much,' he would say, intractably.

A few weeks later a guest reported that a gold shirt stud had vanished from his room, spoiling a set.

'No punggawa this time,' said Bob. 'I'm going to the Dutch police.'

Mr Ogens, head of the Denpasar force, had worked in Bali half his life, and had an eight-inch kris scar in his side to show for it. He had a harsh voice and a terrifying expression.

'Why didn't you call me the first time?' he asked. 'I'll be right down.'

As Ogens' motorcycle stopped near the kitchen, skidding in a half turn, our boys were solemn as owls. After examining the scene of the crime, he dropped his heavy body into an armchair and drank Coca Cola, the favourite soft drink among the Dutch.

'One precaution you haven't taken,' he said. 'You should build a fence around your property. Then, anyone who enters is a trespasser.'

Bob said he would arrange for a bamboo fence with pointed tops but I said we could not have locked gates everywhere. And the main entrance would need a gatekeeper night and day.

'Not at all,' said Ogens. 'Your place now is a thoroughfare. Any kind of fence is a warning to stay out. If you have any more trouble, let me know.'

It would be hard to keep out the people who now drifted past. The Balinese allowed us freely into their villages and took the same liberty with us. We would have to educate the neighbourhood gradually, explain that tourists were peculiar, that they could not bear to be looked at.

The fence was built — and immediately clothes were stolen from the jongoses' room.

Tampa, searching near the fence, found a stolen headcloth and a knife in a leather sheath with the owner's name written on it in Balinese script. Ogens arrested two men, and they were sent to jail for two months.

Number Four seemed an unlucky cottage. One day all its curtains were missing. Leekas found one of them under a mattress with its coins — the Chinese coins with holes in the centre which I used to hang the curtains — cut off.

Two days later, the police led in a sickly boy of fifteen to face his crime.

'Why did you steal the curtains?' Ogens thundered in his official voice.

'For the coins.'

The boy got into our grounds just before dawn by climbing a tree near the fence and jumping over. The coins were worth one-fourteenth of a US cent each. Another jail sentence.

The next case was more serious. A guest lost her diamond ring, and we were sick with worry.

Ogens came to the rescue once more, but this time without result. The boys were becoming used to seeing him around, and had even learned to speak in normal voices in his presence. He was like the Barong — evil but on our side against greater evils. His thundering was like the snapping of the Barong's jaws.

Leekas disappeared for a few hours, and returned to report that an old gardener earning seven and a half guilders a month had been showing ten guilder notes to people in Legian.

The gardener confessed to stealing the ring and selling it to a man in Denpasar — perhaps an agent for the thieves' market in Surabaya. He went to jail for six months. We breathed again, while waiting for the next blow to fall.

A play was being performed on our lawn, a big evening party for new arrivals. I ran into a figure in the dark, a man with a kris in his hand.

'Don't be afraid, Nyonya. It's me, Nyong Nyong. I'm a watchman.'

He was wearing a pink, silk pyjama top a tourist had given him but his legs were bare. The pants of the suit made a turban for his head, with an artificial rose in the centre. He had a touch of make-up on his lips and eyebrows, and the effect was most fetching. But the jacket was so short that a slight breeze or sudden movement might reveal more than was proper. 'What are you wearing underneath?'

He pulled up his jacket and showed me the silk undies I had last seen as he emerged from the surf.

Entertainment in the grounds always drew hundreds of people from nearby villages, along with their little food stalls and small stake gambling tables. On previous occasions some small things had disappeared. Nyong Nyong's radiant expression showed that

his giving up his night with the crowd was its own reward. That would have been fun. This was drama.

'You are a very good jongos,' I said, appreciating his costume more than it was wise to confess. 'Tuan will be delighted when I tell him that you are guarding instead of watching the dancing.'

Even napkins vanished. 'There are almost none left,' said Made Pinatou, our laundryman. Made was a genius in his field. With crude tubs, no bleach, no scrubbing board and only brass flatirons heated with charcoal, he did all the guests' laundry with such skill that all agreed a better laundryman could not exist. When he said anything was lost, it was, and through no fault of his.

Leekas questioned the boys and learned that an old man, the head of a banjar in Kuta, had been seen often prowling near the

▲ Village children put on an informal dance performance for hotel guests. Other village children come to watch. A formal performance would involve much more elaborate costumes.

kitchen at dawn.

A banjar is a co-operative organisation of all married and propertied males in one district of a village. It helps with religious ceremonies and festivals, the building of temples, property protection and other public matters. Bob had sent word to this very banjar a few days before that he would like to become a member and was awaiting its decision. It was unreasonable to suppose that the old man, the banjar head, would stoop to stealing napkins, even if they were of attractive colours.

'I don't believe it,' I said. 'Only a child would take them, for their colours.'

'The old man is a child,' Leekas said. 'A little crazy. I'll look around.'

Soon he returned to say the old man had given one of our napkins to the family which owned the land we had leased for the hotel. Later he traced our napkins all over Kuta and established the old man's guilt. The banjar, to protect him, turned down Bob's application for membership.

We experimented with employing a fulltime watchman, but as the man chosen for the job turned out to sleep all night we rebelled and paid him off.

Luckily, by this time the stealing had come to an end, no doubt because of Ogens' thundering voice and ferocious expression. Jail was an inconvenience but cross-examination by Ogens was a shattering experience.

The second plague was a plague of rats which tried our endurance to the limit, and would have seemed even worse had not Mrs Louise Munson helped us see it through. Mrs Munson, from Philadelphia, and her friend Mrs Stone came to Kuta on a slumming expedition, having been told at the Bali Hotel that two Americans had built native shacks on the beach.

'We expected to find squalid wigwams inhabited by beachcombers,' Mrs Munson told me later. 'When we arrived you were out and we weren't going to wait, but your boys seduced us with

◄ *Nyong Nyong stands guard — wearing a pink, silk pyjama top, with the pants made into a turban decorated with an artificial rose.*

tea and dancing. What delightful people!' They booked in for three days, and eventually Mrs Munson stayed with us for four and a half months.

But she almost left after a week. 'I can't stand it any longer,' she said one morning. 'A rat slept with me last night. He gnawed a hole in the mosquito netting and made a nest on my pillow. He woke me by cuddling against my cheek. I've been up all night — terrified!'

Eventually she decided to stay, however, at least partly because we gave her better protection than the Bali Hotel could offer a rich guest whom all manner of people wanted to meet. Even the famous Walter Spies tried to ingratiate himself with her. Apparently a rat plague was more bearable. We ensured that people she did not want to meet were not received.

Other guests also complained about the plague. I set traps every night, temptingly baited, but the rats ignored them. Poison mixed with food that the rats should have found irresistible was ignored. The rats were interested only in riddling the mattresses, spreading a snow of kapok as they did so.

Every morning I toured the cottages with my sewing basket to patch holes in ticking and batik. Our bed linen on open shelves was stained and had to be washed over and over again until we could get closed cupboards made. My oil paints were eaten. Soap in the washstands was scarred with deep tooth marks every night. Soft grey bodies slid along the rafters in full daylight.

'I think Nyonya brings more rats by not cremating them,' Rankop said. 'When we catch rats, we don't bury them. We always make a good cremation. If you make little towers and burn them, the spirits will not return. Every rat you bury will send a hundred more.'

What devoted servants! They always produced some impractical cure to help us out of trouble.

'I have no time to make towers,' I said. 'Perhaps cats. . .'

'Everyone is having trouble with rats,' Rankop said. 'The villages are full of them. But soon a big celebration in the temple along the beach will send them away.'

➤ A ceremony on Kuta beach. The bamboo platforms are decorated with coloured paper and laden with offerings.

Bob was so shocked at Louise's experience that he sent all gardeners and jongoses hunting with ladders and spiked poles. They swarmed up coconut trees, spearing so many fat rats nesting among the fronds that, at twentyfive cents each, they earned several days' wages.

What made things worse was that much of the damage was done by pregnant rats gathering materials for making nests. There were going to be many more. We concluded that if we had to go through such a plague every year the hotel would not survive. I consoled myself by dreaming of going home, and thinking of the carvings and batiks I would take with me.

'In three days the rats will be gone,' Rankop announced suddenly, after we had endured them for weeks.

'Why do you think so?' I asked.

'Because there will be that temple ceremony I told you about.'

Arriving early, we saw women and girls in ceremonial dress carrying offerings on their heads in and out of the grey stone temple in a clearing among the trees. The stone guardians at the gates were draped in sarongs of black and white checked cloth, with hibiscus flowers behind their ears. The high altars were all laden with offerings, topped by the straw symbols of gods. A priest in white rang a bronze bell and described sacred formulas over a bottle of holy water and baskets of flowers.

We returned to the beach to await the processions. Hundreds of villagers were dotted over the wide expanse of shimmering sand. Every few yards stood a high bamboo platform laden with offerings and fluttering with yellow coconut leaves and coloured paper — beach chairs for the gods. Several of our boys from the hotel joined us. Tampa wore white shorts, flapping shirt tails and a tourist's tropical helmet, while Made Pinatou sported a ragged felt hat and a suit coat.

A procession, with gongs throbbing and cymbals clashing, emerged from the trees and flowed down the steep bank to the sand and out on to the beach. It was led by eight men dressed

➤ *Food — mounds of rice on pieces of banana skin — awaits the feasting which will follow a ceremony. All such preparations are made cooperatively.*

alike and carrying, on shoulder poles, a large, carved casket with a cover like a winged dragon. Their family god was being given an outing by the sea. Twelve men in batik sarongs and red shirts followed, and then came the musicians and a crowd of villagers.

The bearers rushed up to their shoulders into the sea, half ducking their god. They returned and set their casket down. The twelve men removed their red shirts, rolled up their sarongs, and were handed a kris each. One shouted, and each put the point of his kris to his chest and strained to drive it in. Some rolled on the ground and all were shrieking and groaning.

An old man, shaken with trance, darted from the crowd, grabbed a kris and stabbed himself in the chest. Several bystanders jumped on him, forcing the blade away and out of his hands. They led him aside with blood streaming through his shirt. Someone opened it and thrust hibiscus petals into the wound.

After a few minutes, guards grasped the kris men by the hair and disarmed them. An old woman in black sprinkled them with holy water from a preserves jar. Before all had come to their senses, booming gongs announced another procession. Another god was bathed, another kris trance followed. Processions arrived every fifteen minutes, each from a different village, the people in each wearing different colours.

Such self-induced trances occur in a great variety of ceremonies, often spreading to members of the audience. I have already mentioned its place in the barong dance. The usual explanation is that a spirit (not necessarily a good one) enters the body, possessing it to the exclusion of normal awareness. In spite of apparently ecstatic suffering, the person in a trance wakes up as if from sleep, with no memory of the experience and no ill effect other than fatigue. Its purpose is to communicate with the gods and hence to purify. I also suspect, because of its orgiastic character and because the Balinese are repressed by social customs from earliest childhood, that it is an emotional catharsis.

During that ceremony at the beach temple, from offerings inside to the kris trances outside, we could not identify the specific ritual designed to put an end to the rat plague. But from that day their numbers declined, in a week very few were left, and after a fortnight we were free of them for the rest of our time in Bali.

Cooking: Problems and solutions

Running water in the kitchen saved time for more experiments in cookery. As our unattainable aim was to please all nationalities, we were like that man condemned eternally to roll uphill a rock which forever rolled back down again. But we did improve steadily in quality and variety.

When I arrived in Bali, I had cooked for a few years — but over a bathtub in a New York apartment, usually heating something out of a can. Before our buildings were completed, I bought a Boston Cook Book which I examined frequently for recipes for which ingredients were available. We learned to use many substitutes.

Although Java has vast sugar cane plantations, we could not buy raw sugar or molasses and used palm sugar instead. As no gelatine was imported, we used the coarser agar-agar. We used quickly fermenting palm beer to make our bread rise. Because the deer-like Balinese cows give only enough milk for their young, we had no cream — but custard and egg sauces went well with desserts. For the cream in our coffee, we emulsified powdered milk with Australian canned butter.

Fresh meats were beef, pork, suckling pig, scrawny ducks, tough chickens, our own turkeys, occasionally sea turtle, a couple of times goat. New arrivals said hopefully that the beautiful cows they had seen along the road surely provided good steaks and roasts — and we tried not to seem bitter.

Literally, all we dared use was tenderloin, broiled, fried, baked, stewed and hashed. When the cows were slaughtered, the lean meat was cut off in ribbons and lumps, all unrecognisable except the tenderloin. If you bought nondescript bits you had no idea what you were getting and they were very tough — fresh off the hoof.

Bob craved a steak. He went to town with Rankop to see a butcher. He drew diagrams of American cuts, offering a bonus for any kind of steak with bone and fat intact. But when the groceries arrived by dogcart, bare cows' ribs stuck out of a large soap box like cavemen's clubs.

I sent them back with the bill, which was also an insult. Rankop went to town again with more drawings. When the dogcart drove up again, the soap box contained shorter ribs with a two-pound lump of lean meat dangling from the end of each. I considered the matter closed.

But tenderloin, kept in the refrigerator for three days and then grilled, was as tender and good as any in the world and cost only twenty US cents a pound. Shrimps, crayfish, crabs and many kinds of fish came from the sea. Dutch airline pilots brought us oysters from Australia, and newspapers only one day old. Our own turkeys, stuffed and baked, were the same as those from Vermont. The thin native ducks and chickens became tender after slow cooking in the oven for three hours.

We tried every kind of native vegetable, discarding only some which were coarse or bitter, and had also all the European vegetables grown in the mountains for the Dutch community. We had tropical fruits galore.

Rankop and Tampa learned to make cakes, puddings, icecream, jellies and salads. We could buy canned goods from America and Australia and cheeses from Holland. Imported ham, bacon, English marmalade and American coffee were necessary luxuries.

In the kitchen we learned by trial and error.

'We are leaving today,' said two Dutch people who had expected to stay a week. They had been with us only twentyfour hours. 'We don't like the meals,' they added. 'We were given army rations for lunch. We don't have to go to a hotel for that.'

The 'rations' had been browned corned beef hash with poached eggs on top. I had thought it was so good.

Few meals suited all nationalities. Americans preferred light dishes without much fat while the Dutch expected two or three meat courses at a meal, with gravy and soup rich in fat. Americans were thrilled with coffee from home while people from Java liked the bitter extract from their native beans, mixed with hot milk. Americans liked desserts rich and full of flavour. The Dutch preferred starchy, custard-type ones, not so sweet. The kind of toast that Americans liked the Dutch considered burned. Americans liked a breakfast of fruit, toast, bacon and eggs cooked separately, and coffee. The Dutch liked thick slices of plain bread with cold meats, cheese, sardines, kippered herrings. If they had bacon and eggs, the bacon had to be almost raw and cooked under the eggs.

'Look at this,' said the government doctor from Denpasar who had run down for a late breakfast. 'Your cook has spoiled the bacon.'

Three crisp slices sat daintily beside the fried eggs. No one had warned Rankop to cook a Dutch breakfast.

We tried Chinese food, prepared by a cook from a restaurant in Denpasar who arrived with pots and packages. He set bottles of sauces and powders in a row and set about teaching Rankop and Tampa. They obeyed his sing-song orders as he cooked half a dozen dishes at once, limping painfully around the kitchen, pot-bellied and round-shouldered, his ugly face benevolent. Rankop and Tampa were delighted with the diversion and happy with the food as well, which was close to their understanding of what food should be.

'You must remember to write everything down,' I said, 'with the names.'

As the cook turned out one exotic meal after another, the list of combinations grew out of control. No one could pronounce or remember the names. Rankop's notes piled up in confusion, and not even he could understand them. But he and Tampa learned to cook Chinese meals.

Bob's next innovation was cooking himself.

He towered behind a table in the centre of the dining room, wearing a chef's cap and apron several sizes too small. Rankop stood beside him, much smaller and just as serious. Each had a charcoal stove surrounded with platters and dishes of sliced beef,

onions, spinach, bamboo shoots, soya bean cake, vermicelli, sugar, sake (Japanese rice wine) and soya sauce. The dish they would make would be sukiyaki, or a version of it.

▲ *Bob and Rankop (who is fanning the charcoal fire) prepare to cook sukiyaki. Efforts to vary the hotel menu never ceased.*

As Bob set a frying pan on the stove and poured in oil, Rankop did the same. Guests sat around in a circle, so the performance had to be good. Rankop copied his every movement as Bob stirred in the ingredients, adding a pinch of this and a dash of that, mixing and tasting all the while. Side by side the two cooks laboured.

When the two dishes were judged cooked, and as we sat and practised holding chopsticks, Bob changed from teaching Rankop to instructing us. 'Beat the raw egg in the small bowl . . . Rice goes into this dish, sukiyaki into that one . . . Hold your chopsticks so . Dip the meat into the raw egg . . .'

In this manner we spent an hour in ceremonial enjoyment instead of gobbling like westerners. The midday sun, the hot food and the hot sake we drank seemed to envelop us in steam, and I asked the boys to bring fans. They did so, and stood behind fanning and trying to remain dignified through their amusement at our excesses.

Sukiyaki developed into a Sunday custom at the Kuta Beach Hotel, until everything Japanese became unpopular.

Bob was not the only cooking instructor.

'Sometimes guests have good ideas,' I said to Rankop after he had become accustomed to teamwork with Bob. 'People from different countries can teach us. Will you let them work in the kitchen?'

Anyone who seemed promising was invited in. As a result we had new soups, fish entrees, spaghetti sauce and jams. Mrs Bain from Manila, a grandmother who became an air pilot at the age of fiftytwo, taught us to make better use of our homemade ovens, kerosene tins with a door cut in the side and with the bottom covered with broken bricks. Factory-made ones from Java — made for kerosene stoves — melted in the intense heat of the burning charcoal. Later a garage mechanic copied the wreckage in heavy zinc and heat-proof iron bottoms and we had casseroles, puddings and cakes.

Rankop, as determined to please the guests as I was, would not let any process get the better of him. Once I found him on the kitchen floor, holding a bowl between the soles of his bare feet, thrashing the contents with an egg-beater. Tampa squatted opposite him, adjusting a beer bottle on a Rube Goldberg structure

of bricks and boxes. A string led from the neck of the bottle to Rankop's big toe. When he twitched his toe, the bottle tilted and oil dripped from a hole in the cork. Both cooks giggled when I came in, knowing they were not acting their age. Stopping a moment to add oil by hand would have been far less trouble.

'You have made good mayonnaise three times,' Rankop said, jealous of my luck. 'I've had to throw mine away two times.' Now he was taking no chances. If he beat hard without stopping, and used twice the usual amount of egg yolk to compensate for the climate, perhaps it would not curdle. But it was only when he turned the process into a form of entertainment that success was assured.

Neither Rankop nor I ever succeeded in decorating birthday cakes properly. After a bout with ineffectual substitutes, we were always covered with butter, sugar, dyes and perspiration. The lettering and flower designs flattened and ran. Nor did we have any success with fine pastries — we had no pastry flour and few of the tools. I cut gaudy pictures from American magazines and followed directions but the results, though tasty, never resembled the illustrations.

Occasionally something altogether novel turned up. Fried grasshoppers in particular remain in my mind.

The occasion began on a dark night with four of the boys darting here and there, catching grasshoppers which were swarming everywhere. A little later they had been fried a golden brown and the boys were munching them like peanuts. Sabah brought a dish of them for me and a visiting major. I thought they might be as good an appetiser as cashew nuts, if we could get used to them.

I asked Sabah to show how to eat them, and he munched away with a mischievous smile. Had it not been in fun, he could not have been persuaded to eat in our presence. I challenged the major to try this new delicacy.

He hesitated a moment, looking at the folded legs and bulging eyes, and took a handful. 'Good,' he said. 'Rather spicy.' I took his word for it.

◄*Tampa at work with a mixing bowl in the kitchen, wearing one of the new-fangled chef's caps.*

Other oddities which came our way were bee larvae, termites after they had swarmed and shed their wings, and tiny eels about six inches long from the ricefields.

Another experiment began early one morning when I found the kitchen deserted. Three hundred yards up the beach a crowd of men were shouting and digging in the sand. Our jongoses were with them — the whole guilty crew — crawling in and out of a big hole scraped in the sand. They were collecting soft, pearly globes about the size of large hens' eggs.

They were turtle eggs, laid during the night. A fisherman had found the mother's tracks coming from the surf, and the rush was on. The nest had held about forty eggs, of which six eventually came to rest on our kitchen counter. The boys ate some raw, making a hole and squeezing them into their mouths, but I asked for one to be cooked. It became a bland, yellow curdle, tasting of nothing but the butter it had been scrambled in. Bob caught me in the act of eating and hurried out, looking nauseated.

When our new laundry was working — and after some embarrassing incidents in which guests found long, black hairs in their food — we put our cooks into uniform. At first Tampa and Rankop resisted the idea, saying that caps and aprons were 'women's clothes'.

I showed them American magazine pictures of chefs at work, all wearing caps and aprons.

'They are uniforms to show you are good cooks,' I said. 'Caps and aprons will please the guests and the caps will prevent hairs getting in the food.'

I pointed out that the cooks in the illustrations were all big, strong men, and that one of a woman cook showed her in a different cap and apron. Tampa and Rankop agreed to try the uniforms I made on a rented sewing machine — and soon they were wearing them proudly to the Kuta market. Lest anyone should be in doubt where they came from, they painted 'Kuta Beach Hotel' on the boxes tied to their bicycle racks.

In a way I missed seeing the two men cooking in loin cloths, their husky bodies like bronze statues. But the white, starched material of their uniforms also looked good, and we had no more trouble with hairs in the food.

Bing Mueller and Lady Hartelby

Like Louise Munson, Bing Mueller came for three days and stayed for months. These long-term guests gave us a sense of security that we did not get from the quick turnover of round-the-world tourists. If they could put up with us for so long, we must be on the right track as hotel-keepers.

One evening Bing invited all present to have a drink. 'What will everyone have?' he called. 'How about you, Toots? Change your mind and have one on me.'

Lady Hartelby, an intrepid British woman, straightened her jabot with elderly fingers and pursed her lips at the outrageous epithet.

'Really, Bing, you will be my downfall. You know I've had two already. If I keep on, someone will have to put me to bed.'

'That's where I excel, my dear,' said Bing, running his pudgy hand over tightly curled red hair. 'But don't knock yourself out. You and I have a swimming date tomorrow. We must get the best out of those surfboards.'

He was always stimulating in an impersonal, well-bred way, just as his short, round figure was always clad in his idea of what a gentleman of means should wear in the tropics. Made Pinatou liked to launder his linen underwear and sharkskin suits.

Guests surrounded two large coffee tables set out on the lawn. Pressure lamps shed light through wicker and paper shades. The air was cool and misty, the stars half hidden. There was a pungent odour from burning coconut leaves. A fairyland of lights twinkled

Our boys invite hotel guests to dinner.
Such processions were their own idea,
and guests were entranced.

amid the coconut pillars of the dining room and along the long
line of cottage porches beneath the coconut palms. When I
thought how all this must affect newcomers, I took a deep breath
and hoped dinner would not be an anticlimax. By this time the
cooks were so self-sufficient that I often had no idea what was
coming. Then came the sound of distant drumming. Our boys were
preparing a parade to call us to dinner.

Figures walking in single file, led by a bright lamp and with
drumming and tinkling music, came into view, heading towards the
main gate. We heard them turn towards the sea and head back
towards us along the sand. They were making the grand circuit.
The marchers stopped and there came a sudden burst of fire-
cracker explosions, amid hoarse whoops and shouting. Two guilders or more must have gone up in smoke that time. Nothing extra-
ordinary — the boys had done as much for many a parting guest,
chasing away evil spirits which might have troubled him.

The procession formed again and the marchers came up from
the beach and across the lawn. The old gardener led with lamp

held overhead. A boy dishwasher waved a white flag on a pole. Rankop played his xylophone, hung by a cord around his neck. Leekas and Nyongol beat drums with cloth-covered mallets. Tampa and Made Pinatou whanged dishpans with cooking spoons. Sabah and Nyong Nyong clashed lamp reflectors together as cymbals. Costumes varied from chef's caps and aprons to Made's droopy drawers, his old straw sunhat and a bathmat doubled around his waist as protection from the heat of his charcoal irons. The jongoses had decorated their headcloths with flowers and wore yellow sashes, but the old gardener's dusty loincloth still exposed his buttocks and sturdy legs.

Such processions were spontaneous, the boys' own idea. Bob and I had nothing to do with them. The guests were entranced.

At high tide the next day the breakers were more than head high, and it was no time for beginners to go surfing. But plenty of other people were doing so. Some rode their boards in comic poses. Boards leapt and bucked as they were pushed out to sea. Bob

swept on to the sand aboard his big Honolulu board. Most of our boys were in with us, slapping the water with long strokes to imitate Bob's crawl.

Down from the hotel came Lady Hartelby, in a severe black bathing suit, her stern English features lit with determination. My heart sank. Only a few days before she would have drowned in a deep and turbulent spot had not Bob been there to grab her. She could not swim, she was nearing seventy, and now she wanted to go surfing. I tried to dissuade her but the undaunted spirit of the British Empire won.

I demonstrated how she must hold the board in front of her, how to wait and plunge as a wave approached, how she must fling herself flat and then crawl up the board as the current gripped it. Over and over I pushed Lady Hartelby off, until she was carried all the way to shore — more than enough for the first day.

But not enough for Lady Hartelby. Though she was worn out, she struggled back for more, falling under the impact of each wave. I picked her out of the foam, holding her with one hand and her board with the other. The next wave was a beauty. When I pushed her off she disappeared in the spray. A second wave was catching up with her, and I knew that she would not be able to keep her board's nose up. It would dive to the bottom.

My heart racing, I hurried after her. Her empty board was bouncing around but she was nowhere. Then, yards away, I saw her grey head, cap gone and hair streaming over her eyes.

For a week, her meals were served in her room. Patient about being bedridden, she never complained about the ugly green and purple bruises along her thighs where the board had hit her.

Bing called on her each day.

'Awfully tough luck, Toots,' he commiserated. He always got away with calling dignified dowagers 'Toots'. They loved it.

'Oh, I don't mind,' she said. 'I had one jolly good ride. It was worth it. My only regret I won't have time to try it again. How did you catch on so quickly? You're really topping.'

◄*Bob surfing. This photograph is from a postcard he sent to his mother in Los Angeles. 'I'm rather thin here,' he wrote. 'Taken after having malaria. OK now.'*

Bing reddened with laughter and pulled up his shorts to show that he too had a badly bruised thigh. 'I've been through it too,' he said.

I told them that Rankop that day had nearly broken his nose when his board was flung in his face.

Bing left to dress for dinner. Later he appeared in black trousers and short white jacket with a black satin scarf around his waist. It was a lone attempt to raise the tone of the hotel, but a losing battle with Bob who never graced the evening in more than white trousers and an open-neck shirt.

'How are your meals?' I asked the invalid. 'I hope the boys are

↟ A sleepy afternoon in the hotel grounds. These are the cottages which Dutch travel agents derided as 'dirty native huts'.

giving you enough to eat.'

'Entirely too much,' said Lady Hartelby with raised eyebrows. 'I think you should see for yourself.'

As I waited by the kitchen door at eight o'clock that evening, a tray was carried past. The bare wood was heaped in cheap cafeteria style with a whole dinner, from soup to dessert. The quantity was enough for any day labourer. Soup had spilled over the edge of the plate. Meat, potatoes and vegetables were swimming in gravy. Jelly and cake were crushed together in the same bowl. Only a starving man would appreciate such clumsy abundance.

With so much to do, I had overlooked the matter of tray service. The instructions and demonstrations I began then and there lasted several months. For the rest of the week I examined every tray before it was sent to Lady Hartelby.

Before she could walk again, she asked the boys to carry her to the beach every morning. They offered to make a cradle of their hands but she preferred to ride on a surfboard. In her bathing suit, with flowered hat and parasol, she sat in the centre while four jongoses carried the board on their shoulders. Any boys free to do so would run for the drums and a triumphal procession would result, as if she were a raja's wife in her palanquin.

As soon as she was on her feet, Lady Hartelby hastened to catch up with the local developments. Being deprived of direct observation in the case of two young people whom she suspected of living in sin had been a severe trial. They walked on the beach with their arms around each other, and once she had seen them in a furtive embrace. His pyjamas had been seen on her bed but that was not absolute proof since she insisted the laundry boy had made a mistake. But his bedroom slippers had reposed for a whole day on her porch. Had they been left there innocently, after a swim? The story that the two were distantly related and had known each other all their lives was obviously a blind. You could tell by the way they looked at each other.

Interesting items in the lives of the servants had also been neglected while Lady Hartelby was lying in bed. Nyong Nyong had been laid up with a cold, close to pneumonia, and returned to say the local medicine man had advised him to put fences around our altars. Rubbish being carried past in baskets might have offended the gods. Bob asked the carpenter to make the fences but Nyong Nyong's pallor persisted.

'Are you feeling better?' I asked.

'Nearly better,' he said. 'Nearly strong. Soon I shall do a flirtation dance. I promised it to the gods if they would make me well. It will be on the beach so the guests can enjoy it too.'

I told him he still did not look strong and needed codliver oil in his rice.

'It's not necessary,' he said. 'I'm thin because I remember about my wife dying before I came to work here.'

Lady Hartelby came to listen.

'I had so much trouble,' Nyong Nyong said. 'She was going to have a baby in a few days. She was so big.' He gestured to show how big.

'After she died, we had to get the baby out of her. We could not bury the two together.'

'Why not?'

'Because then my wife would turn into a leyak, a demon. She would haunt the graveyard.'

'What did he say? What's it all about?' asked Lady Hartelby, all aglow. I told her.

'So, I put a big, heavy stone on her stomach,' Nyong Nyong said, beginning to giggle, almost hysterically.

Lady Hartelby kept interrupting, asking for translation and explanation.

'Every day I had to examine the corpse. I became sick at the sight. I couldn't eat. After two days the baby still had not come out. So I put another stone, right here.'

He pointed to his diaphragm. Lady Hartelby was breathless. Nyong Nyong was talking in gasps, almost beyond control.

'I was really sick. I waited another two days. The baby didn't want to come out. I put another stone on top. The next day it happened. That's why I'm so thin.'

'I've never heard anything like it,' Lady Hartelby muttered, eyes gleaming, surely sorry she had joined in.

A few days later Bing returned from attending the yearly celebration on Serangan Island, near Sanur. He was exhausted and, though normally immaculate, covered with dried mud. He sank into a chair and called for a whiskey.

'I'm all in,' he said. 'Six helpless women in the boat, and Lady Hartelby not even able to walk. I had to get out and push the boat up the river — in the mud. We'd still be there if I hadn't because the tide was going out fast.'

Tourists are taken to Serangan in little, flat-bottomed skiffs which are poled along a small river winding through jungle growth. The trip is normally made at high tide because the receding water leaves a field of mud. That was where Bing had been.

I told him he would feel better after a bath, and not to worry about having beriberi. Though his face was rosy and his figure well-rounded, he had this notion that he had the disease, and tried to counter it with pills, whiskey and golf every morning on the nine-hole course Bob had built around our grounds.

'I'm all in,' he repeated. 'Never was an athlete. Disapprove of athletics. They enlarge the heart and harden the arteries. Nyongol — one more. The truth is, I'm a coward, afraid of everything — the sea, competition, discomfort. I'm best on my back with child labour fanning me.'

And he retreated to his cottage, where I had rigged up a punka, an Indian fan made of cloth on a wooden frame. It was worked by someone sitting outside pulling rhythmically on a cord. Bing paid children tiny sums to do this for him — hence his reference to 'child labour'.

One afternoon I heard shouts of alarm from the beach. From the upstairs window of our studio I could see people running. Sabah called out that a man had drowned.

On the beach, Luther Davis, one of our guests, was straddling a human form stretched on the sand, working its arms in artificial respiration. I recognised the elderly man who had visited us from the Bali Hotel two days before. His face was bloated and purplish red and his cheek was cold. White froth dribbled from his open mouth. People came running, offering all manner of assistance, but they were too late.

Bing was standing nearby, his breathing laboured. Bob asked what had happened.

'Luther and I were going for a walk,' Bing said, speaking with difficulty. 'See that woman by the road? She was swimming with him — met him at the Bali Hotel. She seems to be afraid to look at him. Hasn't come near him.'

'Anyway, we met her right here. She asked us if we'd seen her friend. Said he had vanished five minutes before. I asked where, and she said, "Out there", pointing to the breakers. I went to look for him. There are some deep spots today and the tide is rough.

'Well, I looked all over. Couldn't see anything. Then I saw the back of a grey head, way out. Took me a while to get to him. He was floating. I turned him over, and put my arm around his chin, and dragged him in. Ugh! I'll never forget that awful face so close to mine. The breakers swept over us so it was hard going. Luther came to help me. The woman has been standing there ever since.'

Bob asked me to take her to one of the cottages and look after her. A doctor arrived, but all he could do was arrange for the body to be taken to Denpasar. Later the woman told me that her friend, whom she had met at the hotel, had told her he was a diabetic and was unable to swim. It had not occured to either of them that his being sick and elderly were sufficient reasons for not venturing out alone. The doctor thought he had probably lost his footing, and the fright had caused a diabetic coma.

At a rather subdued dinner that evening, I asked Bing about what he had been telling us, about fearing the water, about fearing corpses at cremations, about running away from excitement. 'Why didn't you let Luther go into the water while you went for help on land?'

'It was nothing,' Bing said, blushing.

The truth is that Bing, a student of music and a connoisseur of fine living, loved adventure more than he would admit. When World War II broke out he was in the United States. He volunteered for any kind of service, and was on his way to England to become an ambulance driver when his ship was torpedoed and sunk. He was taken prisoner, but finally exchanged in time to die in his own bed of heart failure.

We remember him with affection. I am glad to recall that when he left us he had tears in his eyes and that, in spite of his shyness, he kissed me goodbye. The departure of each sincere guest was deeply sad, for the nature of our business made it most unlikely we would ever meet again.

A selection of neurotics

The remoteness of Bali and accounts of its exotic life cause many seriously disturbed people to go there. Some hope to 'get away from it all', blaming their troubles on causes outside themselves. But most are frankly determined to carry on as usual, searching only for more freedom in which to indulge their eccentricities. We had cases come to stay, and were intimately involved in each as our small and informal household offered us no protection.

With the zeal of novices, we tried futilely to understand and to relieve. Only when our business — our survival in Bali — was threatened did we take the drastic step of turning anyone out. Our patients, as they were in a way, ranged from a harmless, pathetic, suicidal woman to dangerous drunks.

The woman was Maria, from Florida, a pretty, dainty person who was trying to pull herself out of a nervous breakdown while her long-suffering husband stayed home to keep their business going. She had studied and dreamed about Bali and hoped it would make her over. On her very first day she attended a temple festival — only to return saying she could not stand the crowds or the smells.

'Take it easy,' I said. 'You'll get used to everything. You've come halfway round the world just to be here.'

That night, as she had been doing for years, she took strong sleeping medicine. The next morning she appeared with blue circles under her eyes. She had a good figure and small, feminine features, and it was hard to understand why so attractive a girl should feel a failure in life. Her handsome, young husband showed every sign of loving her devotedly, she admitted, but because she had been ill for several years she believed that he was only pretending to do so, out of pity, and undoubtedly was interested in another woman. She was running away from herself.

At lunch she could not eat for sobbing. Bob helped her to her room. She lay on her bed, eyes closed, moaning and tossing about. 'The waves are calling me,' she muttered. 'Let me go. I have to give myself to the sea.' She fell into a kind of coma and lay like a waxen corpse. It was like something out of a bad movie. Bob did not dare leave her that day for fear she would carry out her threat. From then on we watched her constantly, and every night one of the boys slept on her porch.

Though we did everything we could think of to reassure her and make her feel life was worth living, her periods of stupor increased and alternated with bouts of hysterical crying. Bob wired her husband, suggesting he come to Bali to get her as she was not safe alone. This was perhaps beyond his province but he could not take the responsibility any longer. We knew the husband was not well off and that the long trip would put him heavily in debt.

In her first lucid moment, Bob told her what he had done. The prospect of seeing her husband brought her to her senses, after a fashion, and for the next few days she was busy wiring and telephoning Florida, asking him to come . . . and not to come.

'Oh, I'm so glad that I'm going to see him soon,' she said. 'How wonderful!' And an hour later, 'I'm a selfish brute! I can't do this to him. I must wire him not to come.'

He decided to come, and Maria settled down to wait. But the sea tore at her nerves until she was forced to move to the Bali Hotel, where, a stranger in a more impersonal atmosphere, pride made her behave herself. I called on her whenever I was in town, making her promise to bring her husband to Kuta for a visit. But he came and they went, and we never saw him.

The first time Bob was forced to be the tough bouncer rather than the sympathetic host, we were both shaken by the experience. In a conventional hotel, a disorderly person is lost in the crowd or quietly ejected. In our small circle, a drunk was a nuisance and an embarrassment.

John Brown and his wife Ann were nightclub dancers on their first holiday after two years' trouping through the Orient. Ann, a lovable and cheerful girl with round, pink cheeks and dark, fluffy hair, invented the numbers and made their costumes. Her husband could not forgive her for being the brains of the team. He was pleasant enough at first but his lean face showed lines of discontent.

As Ann was planning some new acts, incorporating suggestions from the Balinese, we engaged Lotring — perhaps Bali's finest musician and dance teacher — for her, along with his wife and daughter as assistants.

A space was cleared in the dining room. The wife or the little daughter danced slowly, showing one step at a time, while Ann followed with Lotring holding her wrists from behind. One of the boys played the accompanying tune on Rankop's xylophone. Ann made phenomenal progress. Her hands and arms followed the sudden, angular movements while she tramped up and down, her bare feet pointing outwards and her knees bent. She was unlearning most of her conventional schooling.

Meanwhile, John drank steadily.

'He never drinks while he's working,' Ann said apologetically. 'A little on days off. But recently he's taken a bit more.'

At the end of a week, John was beyond control. I pitied Ann. As John grew worse, he more openly insulted her.

'I'm the man of this family. I keep the money right here,' he proclaimed, striding around the room and slapping his hip pocket. 'If she wants it, she has to ask for it. And I give it to her or not, as I please.'

When Ann begged him not to have another drink, he swore at her abominably and told her to go to their room.

One night John would not go to bed. We left him alone with his

▲ *Old people were just as photogenic as the young.*

223

head lolling over a glass. In the morning, Ernest, a young YMCA worker seeing life for the first time, told me of a sociological study — as he called it — he had made the night before.

About midnight John had called him to get up and dress. He was on his way to Kuta village to look for a woman and wanted a companion to witness his prowess. The two had zigzagged down the dark drive, Ernest holding John's arm to steady him. In Kuta, the village was asleep. John went to a gate and called loudly in English, 'Hey, you there! Who's inside? I want a woman, d'you here? Get me a woman or I'll come in and get one myself.'

No answer. John stumbled to the next gate and called again. Same words. Same response.

Finally John walked boldly through a gate and the two men found themselves in a maze of shadowy huts. Dogs raised an uproar. Finally an old crone appeared, understood the purpose of the visit, and pointed to a broken-down hovel.

Inside, a woman was lighting a small kerosene lamp. She turned towards them, in the dim light, and motioned them to enter. Both men shrank from her coarse face, shrunken breasts, hair hanging dankly over her shoulders. The hut smelt of garlic and stale coconut oil. Its only furnishings were a bare, slat bed with a filthy pillow and a few rags in a box. This was too much, even for John, and the two turned and ran.

The next morning Ann, who no doubt knew something of what had happened and whose eyes were swollen, asked us not to give her husband another drink, no matter how he urged. She had thrown away his last bottle of gin and hoped he would sober up before he could get more from Denpasar.

As Bob and I had to go to Denpasar on pressing errands, we told Rankop to go to Kuta in the event of trouble and phone us at the grocery shop. He did so, his voice hoarse with fright.

'Send Tuan home at once,' he called. 'Tuan Mabok (Mr Drunk) is very angry. He climbed up the kitchen wall to get into the liquor closet. We pulled him down by the pants. He fell into the pots and the big bag of rice. Everything is all over the floor. He says he will beat up the jongoses if he doesn't get a drink. He says he wants

◄ *A boy arrives at a cottage with a tea tray for our guests while another two entertain with music on their drums.*

Tuan Koke right away — to fight with him.'

We dashed home at full speed, scattering chickens from the roadway. John was pacing the porch, his face like thunder. Bob spoke first.

'I hear you want to pick a fight with me, John. We've stood enough, so pack up your things and go.'

John stood rigid, fist clenched, like a cornered animal.

'Stand up. I'm going to fight you,' he said. 'You can't put me out because I'd decided to leave before you came back. What kind of a dump is this, anyway? Who are you?'

I found Ann crying, trying to pack.

'Let me help you,' I said. 'I'm so sorry. You've done your best. It isn't your fault.'

John was waiting for me in the dining room, his face pinched and yellow. I launched into an angry lecture about how obnoxious he had become. He made monkey faces at me, sticking out his tongue, squinting, pulling his lips down and baring his teeth. I might as well have been talking to a gargoyle.

'You can't do this to me. You can't put me out,' he said. 'I'm going because I want to. You'll never hear the end of this. It's going to cost you thousands and thousands of dollars. I'm going to make so much trouble for you that you'll regret this day till the end of your life.'

He raged on like this as he paid his bill, as he and Ann waited for their taxi, and even as they drove off he stuck his head out the window and shouted threats.

They drove to the Satria Hotel in Denpasar, where John's condition was so obvious that the manager refused to admit them, and they went to a guilder-a-night Chinese hotel instead. The next day they took the dawn bus to Java.

Another appalling drunk, Morgan, late one night sent for his chauffeur.

'Please go to bed,' I pleaded. 'What's the use of driving when there's nowhere to go? Everyone is sleeping by now.'

His chauffeur, Ketut, handsome as a young deer, appeared with his hair mussed and eyes half closed.

'So there you are,' Morgan said in English. 'Now you can go back to sleep. I just wanted to check up on you.'

Ashamed and embarrassed, I told Ketut that he could go, that I would explain in the morning. I knew that no Balinese would stand for such treatment, so Ketut would be leaving in the morning.

Half an hour later Morgan sent for Ketut again. The same thing happened again. Morgan's beaky nose, slit mouth and red skin reminded me of a bird of prey.

'I pay him,' he said. 'A chauffeur is supposed to be here when I want him.'

Ketut left and Morgan searched in vain for another driver. No one would take the job. Morgan decided to drive himself. On his first trip he drove into a food stall. No one was hurt. He handed out a fistful of money to pay for the damage.

A couple of nights later he woke me, just to talk. He was lonely. He had inherited a fortune and had no incentive to work. At forty-five he had nothing to live for, as even spending money had become a bore. He asked for the key to the liquor closet. When I refused to give it to him he got in his car and raced off recklessly.

Driving like that, one night he turned his car over. I learned about it when I heard an engine roaring early in the morning, and found some of our boys trying to push Morgan's car out of soft sand where it had fetched up. They told me that 'Tuan Mabok' was in his room, asleep with blood all over the sheets. His window was broken.

Staggering home after crashing his car, he had forgotten that two boys always slept in the dining room to help people who came in late. Finding his room locked, he had put his fist through the glass to get in.

On another occasion he went to Kuta with a wad of one guilder notes and handed them out to everyone in sight. The villagers were amused and puzzled but took the crazy man's money anyway. At times he paid the villagers to drink beer, though they did not like it, and to listen to his long monologues in English. It seems that dominating a poorly dressed rabble of market women, fishermen and coolies provided momentary relief from frustration.

He left us saying he was going to travel around the world again, and then would return to build a house next to our hotel. Six months later some of his baggage turned up. We waited, hoping he would not show up. Months passed, until we learned that he had been sent home from another Far Eastern port, with a doctor to watch him all the way. But he never reached home. One day, walking on deck, he eluded his doctor and leapt into the sea. The ship searched for hours but could not find him.

In the early days we put up with a lot because we felt that we needed the business, and feared that too firm a hand would give us a bad name. Later we developed a sense of self-preservation. When roisterers roused our boys at midnight, demanding drinks and calling for young women to join them, Bob would send them on their way with a few sharp and well-chosen words.

When a woman who had won our affection drank herself into a stupor every evening, we were not too soft-hearted to find her a cottage in Denpasar and invite her to move in. At times people chronically at odds with the world were encouraged to enjoy the beauties of Java.

This was to protect our other guests from nuisances, and also to protect ourselves. We needed our time and strength for routine work. An average day had quite enough complications without the demands of neurotic guests as well.

For instance, while sewing curtains which were needed immediately, I would be called to greet new arrivals, and have to spend an hour reassuring them that our water was not polluted, that we served plenty of vegetables, that we used butter and not margarine in cooking, and that there were neither sharks in the water nor snakes in the shrubbery. I would hurry back to finish the sewing, only to be told someone had put a foot through a mosquito net. On my way there with my sewing basket, a jongos would cycle after me to answer a telegram. Made Pinatou would tell me of an emergency in the laundry which demanded more hands. And the refrigerator would break down, so someone had to go to Denpasar urgently for ice. In his sphere Bob was just as busy as me, attending to everything from broken waterpumps and people who wanted money from the safe to demands for tour guides and instruction in surfboard riding.

A friend wrote from New York, bent on stopping us from becoming beachcombers.

'Come on home, you lotus eaters,' she urged. 'Come home before the empty life on a tropical beach gets you.'

I do not remember just what I answered, but I surely told her we were using all our faculties and needed a dozen more.

Full house

The dry season of 1939 was the busiest of our five years of hotel-keeping. We were crowded from June to November, with the exception of a few days of panic when war was declared in Europe, and we referred so many people to the Bali Hotel that Bob called it 'our annex'.

On one memorable occasion we had three or four guests in each of our four double cottages, the two single cottages had extra men in their porches, and three people occupied our original bamboo rooms, now leaning picturesquely. Bob and I had moved to the office and its back room to give the studio to people who had written weeks in advance. In one day alone we turned down twenty tourists — and gave in after dark when two married couples said they would have to sleep in their cars. All we could offer were the four couches in the dining room, which were gratefully accepted.

We felt ourselves really successful. We even had a telephone, not so long before an unthinkable convenience. We had had our application in for more than two years, and for virtually all that time had been stymied by the phone company's refusal to tap the existing line from Denpasar to the tiny government office in Kuta. The system did not permit party lines. If we wanted a phone, we would have to pay for several hundred poles and six miles of wire to bring our own line from Denpasar.

A new Controleur, Mr Berger, solved our problem. Two people

Dinner in the hotel grounds was relatively informal but visits to
Bali's religious and cultural sights demanded careful attention to

*respectful attire. Note the men behind with jackets and solar
topees. But a well-intentioned experiment with Balinese attire was
a disaster.*

had drowned in Kuta and there would surely be more emergencies. One day soon a telephone could make the difference between life and death. The government office was open for only a few hours in the morning while we rolled around the clock. Soon workmen in drooping trousers were digging holes, setting up iron poles and stringing wires on them. Before we knew it a telephone sat on Bob's big, professional, second-hand desk.

Leekas called all his high-caste friends who lived anywhere near a phone, speaking the most elaborate Malay or the most devastatingly polite Balinese, flattering his hearers and ensuring future service. Tampa and Rankop were delighted, because now they could drop all pretence of keeping lists of what the kitchen needed. Why bother, when you could phone ten times a day for any little thing? Now it was the shopkeeper's task to keep a list of what we needed. He complained but it made no difference.

With so many guests, we were all desperately busy, and our experienced boys were to be valued above gold — yet at this time one of our best had to be dismissed. Nyongol charmed everyone with his good looks and pleasing manner. We assumed he was permanent, but his yielding ways lost him to us.

One morning I found him with his lip torn and swollen.

'What is it?' I asked.

'It is nothing.'

'Did you fall down?'

'It is just . . . a little accident.'

Giggles from the kitchen told me it was more than that.

'It is just . . . my wife tried to kill me with a kris. I grabbed it. The handle hit my lip.'

The story came out slowly. I learned from various sources that Nyongol had been making up to a woman of high caste, the most serious offence he could have committed in the old days, and still grounds for divorce. For such an offence, in the old days, he would have been thrown off the cliff at Bukit.

A few days later he asked Bob for a lift into town to see his family. They wanted him to divorce his wife, and a few days later he did so. I asked how much it had cost. He said twentyfive cents.

Within a short time, Nyongol found another woman, as hard and calculating as he was weak and easy-going. After agreeing with her on the time and place, he made arrangements to kidnap her, the cheapest and simplest form of marriage. Nyongol planned carefully because the abduction must not be seen by any member of the bride's family. If the act were observed, she would have to be freed and another attempt made later.

Bob was asked to lend his car, and was so excited at the prospect of romantic adventure that he insisted on driving. But the presence of a white man so frightened the girl that she refused to get in the car, and Nyongol had to go for her the next day on his bicycle.

He took her to a friend's home, where the bride and groom spent three days and nights in seclusion. After the third day they were considered married, and a simple ceremony followed. There would be more pretentious ceremonies later when money had been saved.

We went to Nyongol's little celebration in flag-draped cars. An unholy din came from the car packed with our boys. We took bottles of lemon pop and water glasses as presents. The bride sat in a torn and soiled blouse and faded sarong. Her long hair was wound untidily in a dirty towel.

'Why does your wife wear old clothes?' I asked the blushing groom. 'You said she is from a rich family.'

'A good wife does not care how she looks. She must not spend money on herself. If she dresses poorly she is thinking only of being a help to her husband.'

We drank to their prosperity and fertility.

Nyongol was supposed to come back to work that night. The jongoses had agreed that three days was long enough to get married. But he asked for another night, and got it. The next day he sent a message that he would not be back for another week.

Nonetheless, when he returned we were overjoyed to see him, not only because his competence made him invaluable but also because we were so fond of him. His new wife was determined to get him away, however. She wanted to support him herself while he helped in her food stall. He was battling a woman who was set on making him a servant in her family instead of her going to his home. Entirely in her power, he began taking still more time off.

The end came abruptly. 'You received five guilders from guests who were leaving,' I said. 'You have not put half in the bank. Leekas, Sabah and Nyong Nyong received five guilders each, and they have given their half.'

This was a custom the boys had inaugurated. Routine tips were pooled while personal gifts of money were divided, half for the person who received it and half for the pool, or bank, to be shared out at the end of each month.

'I did not receive a present,' Nyongol insisted with eyes downcast.

The other boys were angry. They remembered other times that Nyongol had come to the kitchen with empty hands after a guest had left. Now they understood why. Bob and I begged him to play fair, explaining that if he could cheat the boys no one would trust him not to steal from the guests. We told him how much we liked him and needed him.

Alone in the office, later, we had to say one of the hardest things to tell anyone you are truly fond of.

'I was mistaken,' Nyongol said with blanched face when he realised what was happening. 'I did receive five guilders but I forgot. I have so much to remember. Now it comes back to me. I will never do it again, I swear.'

'You will have to go,' Bob said. 'The other jongoses refuse to work with you.'

His wife had won.

Another emergency developed when Wayan, inexperienced but essential now that Nyongol had gone, asked for a day off. His child had been hit a glancing blow by a car mudguard. No harm was done but Wayan insisted that he had to keep a fire going all night at the scene of the accident to placate the gods.

I offered to send him to the scene in the car and to bring him back after he had built his fire and left his offerings.

'Adoh! Adoh!' he said. 'My child! The gods will be angry.'

I offered to pay for extra offerings. While this was going on, guests were calling me, boys were running about with trays of drinks, the kitchen was a traffic jam.

'Think about it for a few minutes,' I said. 'Your boy was not even hurt, so five guilders is enough for offerings. Ask the jongoses if I am right.'

Wayan crept away with his head bowed under the weight of decision, and returned upright to say all the boys had agreed he need not stay with the fire all night. A priest would fix things for him. He returned in time to help serve dinner.

There was to be a big religious event in a temple in Denpasar. 'No one will be admitted who is not in traditional Balinese dress,' Leekas translated the notice on the wall.

'Does this mean our guests must dress in Balinese clothes?' I asked.

'It means that if they do not they may not be admitted,' Leekas replied.

I told our guests what would be expected of them. Six people decided to go. Leekas brought out a mound of the best dress-up garments he could borrow, some interwoven with gold thread and some overlaid with gold flower designs. I added a sarong shining with yellow silk thread and some headcloths of handwoven lace. Leekas had krisses for the men and flowers for everyone.

When we gathered on the front lawn after dinner, we could hardly contain our amusement at each other's comic appearance and discomfiture. The jongoses were still busy tying sarongs and scarves over layers of western clothing. An elderly professor of mathematics had settled on a harmony of burnt orange and yellow which he thought becoming with his grey hair, blue eyes and stocky figure. White and tan shoes and green socks showed beneath his sarong and he could not get used to the kris handle projecting over his left shoulder.

A mining engineer from Oklahoma was so tall that several inches of white trousers showed, and he had trouble with a hibiscus behind his ear and a headcloth which would not stay put. Leekas was busy among the women, tying, pulling and pinning, trying to persuade them that the brilliant colours they were not accustomed to really suited them. 'I guess we're going to give the Balinese a treat tonight,' said one. I hurried them into the cars before they lost their nerve.

At the temple, as we plunged into a milling crowd of hundreds, the gamelan music stopped. Even the priest's bell stopped ringing. A procession of women carrying offerings on their heads broke formation and came to see what was happening. As we were led to a pavilion, we became the show. Freaks in a circus could not have been exhibited to better advantage. The celebration would

continue until dawn so there was plenty of time for a sideshow such as ours.

Some among us were already near breaking point when three Dutch men in European dress came through the gate. No one paid

▲ Tampa, with cooking pot doubling as a helmet, dances as he imagines a cripple would dance.

them the least attention. When they caught sight of us, they squinted in deep disapproval and turned away. That was the last straw. We forced our way out through the crowd, perhaps with a few shreds of dignity remaining — but very few. We had seen very little of the Balinese performance, but the Balinese had certainly enjoyed ours.

A Frenchman, Henri Lyons, who stayed with us about this time provided another diversion, at first for the jongoses, then for a much wider audience.

'Tuan Number Six is in the sea,' Sabah said, the whites of his eyes shining. 'He has only one leg.'

'The other is made of wood,' I said. 'He lost a leg in the big war.'

Sabah, still breathing fast from his run to the kitchen with the big news, scurried on to Number Six. Soon he was back spreading still more news, this time about an amazing artifice with long straps. One by one the boys ran to the cottage to see, taking care to run behind the cottages, out of sight from the beach, while Sabah stood ready to give the alarm if the owner returned.

'Wonderful! Wonderful!' they said on returning, each one demonstrating his idea of how the artificial leg should be attached. When Tampa returned last, he put a cooking pot on his head and danced like a man whose leg gave way every few steps. It was not unkind, for just such an injury might be clowned in any of their dramas.

'I don't mind,' Henri said when I told him. 'I'll show it to them so they can see how it works. They're very nice boys. In fact, I'd like to give them some better entertainment. A real Balinese party, dinner and show afterwards, whatever they like. Tell them to arrange it and I'll give them the money.'

Then he strapped on his leg while a circle of fascinated jongoses looked on.

Organising the party took days. Many questions had to be answered. Was it better to pay three guilders more for the best shadow play and economise on the flirtation dance? Would roast pig be more economical than turtle? Should they serve arak or the cheaper palm beer? Finally they decided on a pork dinner for sixteen friends and certain entertainments on the beach afterwards. It

would cost forty guilders, about US$22.

When the day arrived, activity began early. People arrived to roast suckling pigs over an outdoor fire. More came with baskets of cooked rice and vegetables. Three companies of players assembled on the beach. The screen for the shadow play was put up, a square of white cloth lashed to a wood frame on a high platform, with a slanting roof overhead. Several hundred people came wandering in from neighbouring villages. Women arrived with the food stalls on their heads, and settled down to selling snacks and drinks.

Dinner was served to the invited guests and the shadow play began, a tale of gods and heroes, villains and clowns outlined by puppets manipulated between a flaming lamp and the white screen. Musicians provided background music and the dalang, or puppeteer, supplied dialogue, commentary and sound effects. The

crowd was enthralled by a story as fast and slick as any movie thriller.

A flirtation dance followed, with music as strident as the calliope of an old-fashioned circus. The dancer, a girl of eleven or twelve, her powdered face expressionless but her eyes flashing, enticed man after man to dance with her. One parodied the whole affair, prancing like a contortionist and drawing shouts from the audience when he brushed the girl's lips with his. Bob also took his turn, throwing his lanky body about with comic abandon and using his hands as paddles rather than attempting the girl's intricate co-ordinations.

▲ *Three dancing girls. Virtually every Balinese child has opportunity to learn to dance, and if he or she shows promise to become a star soloist. There is never any shortage of performers.*

An opera followed, with players entering slowly through a curtain strung on a pole. When they got into full swing, the clowns joking loudly and the high castes singing in high, choked voices, we gave out and went to bed. As the show lasted till daylight, the boys were asleep on their feet the next day.

'I've given all kinds of parties,' Henri said. 'But never have I entertained so many. There were four hundred people there, I believe. It was a wonderful evening. And the cost — it was nothing.'

By the end of the season, when business began to decline, we were away ahead financially. The war in Europe was making inroads into the number of people touring the world. Without it we would not have been able to build cottages fast enough. Even so, intoxicated by months of full houses, we blindly built two more double cottages with tiled bathrooms. Blindly, because we could not see that the war would spread, perhaps even to Bali.

▲ *Bob takes his turn in the flirtation dance, throwing his lanky body about with comic abandon.*

Medical complications

By the end of 1939 we had achieved the germ of a farm which was entertaining, if not profitable. We had a flock of sixty turkeys, which the Balinese called 'ayam baris', the first word meaning 'chicken' and the second a dancer who struts just like a turkey. Mario brought us our first pair from Tabanan. We had chickens, ducks and pigeons as well, though we could not bring ourselves to eat the pigeons. For pets we had a demented goose always under our feet and a cockatoo who shared our meals, ruined our furniture and had to be taught how to fly.

To complete the farm idea, Bob continued gardening — but against odds which seemed insurmountable. He brought in tons of rich earth, made leaf shelters to protect plants from the sun, sent to the United States as well as Java for seeds, engaged men to carry oceans of water, and finally tried hydroponic culture in specially made troughs.

Except for excellent tomatoes, some eggplants and a few gardenias, his efforts were in vain. He figured that the eggplants cost two guilders each and that the gardenias were priceless. Haunted by the facts, he eventually discarded the noble theory of self-sufficiency, and put up with vegetables from the market and flowers from the hedges. The vegetables were cheap and the flowers were free.

With the same zeal that Bob had poured into gardening, I tried to win over our boys and their families to the spells cast by modern doctors and the magic of certain foods. My results were just as meagre. While Bob planted seeds that never developed, I tried to impart new ideas to people who had no words to express what I was trying to talk about.

Quinine and the pesticide we used to kill wood borers were both 'ubat', or 'medicine'. This same word had to cover also vitamins and minerals as well as castor oil and household ammonia. Germs were 'small animals' whose alleged existence could be discounted as I had no microscope with which to prove my claims.

The most difficult family problem was Tampa's wife when she was tormented by hives. One day a delegation of scandalised neighbours called Tampa to come at once. His wife was in their yard, naked, dashing water over herself, crying. Her hysterical fits increased. Tampa did not dare leave her alone so all cooking fell to Rankop.

I visited them, and asked if they knew what the sickness was.

'Leyaks perhaps,' said Tampa, referring to the spirits which haunt graveyards and crossroads. In two and a half years Tampa had matured from a careless lad to a responsible husband.

'The medicine man says I built our house facing the wrong way,' he continued. 'Evil spirits can't find their way out. I must make another, facing north.'

I told him that his house had cost him fifteen guilders, that it was a good house and that he had no money to throw away. I asked him to let me take his wife to a modern doctor.

'She won't go,' he said. 'She says she would rather die. I must take her back to her family in Bangli. I can't help her and I can't work while she's here.'

I drove them both to Bangli, twentyfour miles away. Rankop spent his hard-earned money on a new house, at right angles to the first. His wife returned in better health but soon relapsed. I felt her trouble was anaemia probably aggravated by frustration because she did not have initiative enough to keep herself occupied. For a time she collected eggs but Rankop refused to buy them as she was quarrelling with his wife, next door.

The medicine man told Rankop that she must have still another house, at yet another angle. I told Rankop about the times modern medicine had cured him when he had malaria and a temperature of 105 degrees. But even a husband's authority had certain limits and his wife refused to submit to foreign magic.

While Tampa was buying bamboo for his third house, Rankop came to us in a panic. His baby boy was unconscious. He had had a fever that morning and I had given Rankop an atabrine tablet, telling him to cut it in three and get one of the pieces into the baby any way he could.

Bob and I found his worn and frightened wife with the child in her arms. Bob held a flashlight to the child's half open eyes but they did not close and the pupils remained large. His fluttering pulse was alarmingly feeble. We rushed him to the hospital in Denpasar, where an injection brought him around in two hours. In a few days he was completely recovered, and Rankop was converted.

Another crisis developed when Made Pinatou, our peerless laundryman, developed an ulcer in his groin. As he was irreplaceable, we dared not let him go to a medicine man. We bullied him into going to the hospital, and while he was there made shift to cope with the laundry as best we could. The jongoses did some when they could find time, some went to a primitive Chinese laundry in Kuta, and I took guest's clothing to a better one in Denpasar. Every afternoon I ironed table linen.

When Made returned, bent and hobbling, the ulcer was still ugly. New guests making the rounds of the buildings might surprise him in his laundry, sitting in a tub of hot water to lessen the pain. Finally, sick and discouraged, he escaped to his village and its medicine man.

After two more weeks of disorganisation, we went to see him. He was thinner and stooped like a cripple. By a ruse, pretending that we only wanted him examined, we got him back to the hospital. We knew the doctor would scare him into staying, and he did.

I visited Made often as he lay on a board bed with a grass mat underneath, a blanket and a pillow. One day I asked the high caste male nurse who had helped us with Munik what Made's trouble was. Did he have 'woman sickness', or venereal disease? The nurse thought he had.

Syphilis and gonorrhea rates are high in Bali, even higher than

in Java, although the people have developed some resistance and
seldom show acute symptoms. I had tried to impress on our boys
that 'woman sickness' was not spread by women alone, as they
thought, but that men could infect their wives and unborn
children. They looked at me with glazed eyes, just as when I tried
to explain the changes of the moon — everyone knew it was re-
gularly eaten by a monstrous head.

↑ *Made Pinatou, our peerless laundryman, sits in hot water to
lessen the pain of a persistent ulcer in his groin. I unjustly
accused him of having venereal disease — unjustly because he
was too shy for any adventure which could have produced such a
result.*

'The nurse tells me you have woman sickness,' I said to Made. 'You have two good wives. Are they not enough for you? Do you have to sleep with the bad women in Kuta?'

'Believe me,' he said with the utmost sincerity, 'I've not slept with any women except my wives. I've been working in Kuta only a short time. I don't know the women there so I wouldn't have the courage to sleep with them.'

I knew he was speaking the truth. The men of Bali reserve all freedom for extra-marital relations, but Made was indeed too shy to exercise this liberty. And as it turned out, the nurse was wrong and we were able to take Made back as soon as he was cured.

Because treatment for a minor epidemic among the boys was diverting, it met with no resistance. They clattered around on wooden sandals, elevated to a high caste level. Dutch people from Denpasar appeared shocked by this breach of custom.

'They all have athlete's foot from standing in spilled dishwater. Bob is treating them and wants them to keep their feet dry,' I explained.

At the same time, as they lined up for Bob, I tried to treat the white patches of a different fungus which mars the sleek brown bodies of so many Balinese. We expected occasional discolouration but this was abnormal.

Finally, when Sabah's feet showed deep clefts and fungus patches persisted among half a dozen boys, a government doctor was called in.

'Your servants aren't getting enough vitamins,' he said. 'Until they do, you can't cure them. What do they eat?'

I explained that I gave Rankop money for their meals and he bought what they liked. In the morning they wanted only strong coffee with sugar. At noon they had polished rice with oddments from a food stall. The evening meal was much the same. Between meals they sucked flavoured ices sold by a hawker who carried them in a thermos flask. Sometimes a boy would bring packets of beans or rice strewn with palm sugar back from Kuta.

'That's not enough,' the doctor said. 'They must have three good meals a day — meat, eggs and green vegetables with the water left from cooking. Give them papaya at breakfast and kacang hijau (a green bean rich in vitamins) in the middle of the morning.'

It sounded good in theory but could not have been put into practice without a government order and the power of the police. No one wanted fruit — fruit was for eating only when bought at a stall during some gathering. Everyone was willing to add rolls from a Chinese bakery to morning coffee, but as they were made from white flour they had none of the 'medicine' the doctor ordered. As for the kacang hijau, it was cooked and set out for them every morning — only to be mixed with a mass of sugar or to be entirely refused. The boys ate the meat and eggs but cheated on the water vegetables had been cooked in.

By this time Tampa and Rankop, our cooks, had acquired our tastes and polished off everything left over, including chocolate pudding and coconut cake which should have been kept for the next day.

One day I invited the boys to look at them. 'Have you noticed that Rankop and Tampa are healthier than the rest of you?' I asked. 'They are, and it's because they eat everything. We eat more different foods than you do, so we get more "medicine".'

I asked Rankop, the sturdiest of them all, scarcely bothered even by malaria, what he had eaten as a child.

'My family was so poor that we lived mostly on vegetables,' he said, his eyebrows raised in self-pity. 'Rice was expensive in my village.'

'There!' I said, grasping at a straw. 'That's what I've been telling you. The "medicine" in vegetables helped Rankop grow up strong.'

The boys listened, just as politely expressionless as when I told them that the world was a globe revolving around the sun. I even demonstrated with oranges. But they knew the world was flat and that rice was the magic sustainer of life. No one could ask more than a full stomach.

The new diet was continued, however, with a rising standard of good health. Without ever believing in the connection between the two, the boys finally learned to eat breakfast, to eat fruit and even to drink milk when recovering from malaria. They told each other they did so just to keep me quiet.

Then I fell ill. I had just come back from a friend's cottage in the mountains at Kintamani where I had had my second holiday in four and a half years of being assistant everything in a hotel. For three days Bob nursed me while at the same time trying to take care of a house full of guests — the Christmas rush of 1940. By phenomenal good fortune we were never both sick at the same time. When Bob had malaria or dysentery, I was well. Now it was his turn to look after me.

While I was alone on the third day, pain in the region of my appendix was so acute that I called for help — but could not shout strongly enough to be heard. I tried to inject myself with morphine but the needle broke in my thigh and I could not walk across the room for another. Bob returned, and called Dr Roestam from Karangasem, half the length of Bali away.

He told me I had peritonitis and that he would try to find some sulfanilamide in Denpasar.

'I believe we have some,' said Bob. 'One of our guests left us his medicine kit.'

He ran out, and returned with a bottle of the new drug which would save my life. Even so, the next twelve days were a nightmare of pain and occasional delirium. Eventually I felt the way a corpse looks. I was as weak as a trickle of water.

'I think I may die,' I told Bob during one of his hurried visits. 'I used to be afraid of death but now it seems so simple. One more degree and you're gone — that's all. But I like living with you. We've had wonderful years together, especially in Bali. I'll try to hang on.'

'Cheer up, old girl,' Bob said, rising to the occasion. 'You'll be OK.'

Then he patted my arm absentmindedly while telling me that

the Christmas turkey was underdone and that some guests had complained because he had not had time to write out the breakfast menu.

Dr Roestam wanted me to go to Surabaya where the hospital was better equipped than the Denpasar one. Bob was able to charter a twelve-passenger Lockheed for one thousand guilders (US$550) for the round trip. A motor van, once part of an eccentric attempt to help Bali's starving mongrel dogs, had been converted into an ambulance. It was waiting at the door. All the boys watched in silence as I was carried out, expecting never to see me again. Morphine made the springless old vehicle seem soft as a feather bed. On the plane, Bob and Dr Roestam were reassuring blurs.

In hospital in Surabaya, doctors drained what Dr Roestam had reassuringly described to me as 'an abscess as large as a grapefruit' in my abdomen. I was in that hospital for six wretched weeks, two months' convalescence back in Bali followed — and then I flew back to Surabaya to have my appendix out.

My references to malaria and other ailments, and my own narrow escape from death, must sound like a formidable warning against living in the tropics. This is not the impression I mean to give. Most travel accounts are too glossy. I am only trying to be honest.

We knew many Dutch people who had spent most of their lives close to the equator without ill effects. Some never got malaria and all who did, like us, recovered. If malaria is treated immediately, it usually subsides in a few days if you are otherwise in good health. If you stay home, you may contract something worse. Bob's dysentery had been contracted years before our trip started and my broken appendix could have happened anywhere.

In case any of my readers plan to venture to that remote island of their fantasy, they do not need to fear the disintegration which popular fiction so often paints as the white person's eventual fate in the tropics. Quite the contrary. United States Army statistics show that white men can do hard physical work for months on end in intense heat and dampness if modern medical precautions are taken. If I could do it over again, I would wager a good sum that I would come out in good health.

Old dances and new

While Donald Oenslager, a well-known stage designer studying Balinese dancing and drama, and his wife Zorka were staying with us, they asked if they could see the island's newest performance, the janger. It was so new it was still developing. We invited three budding companies — whose members we had heard rehearsing their numbers for weeks as they strolled past the studio — to make their first public appearances on our lawn.

The janger, with boys and girls taking part and with singing as well, is quite different from all other Balinese dances. It attracts moppets from five to twelve years old who form a club with one of them as treasurer, an adult as supervisor, and helpful relatives and others to provide the music. Twelve girls sit in two rows of six facing each other, and two rows of boys fill the other sides of a hollow square.

The girls wear crowns decorated with flower-like creations mounted on thin wires. These vibrate and glisten with every move. As the girls sit on their heels, colourfully dressed, with arms swaying, fingers moving, heads sliding from side to side, eyes rolling and flashing, they are no longer the inconspicuous children who roam the village but glamorous idols with shimmering halos.

The boys dress in clownish combinations of bright red shirts and black shorts with sneakers on their feet and white chalk smeared carelessly on their faces. Black moustaches of all shapes and sizes are painted on their hairless upper lips. Around their necks are wide collars of black velvet decorated with beads and sequins, like cast-off circus trappings.

All jangers are basically the same, with endless variations. One company visits another to get ideas for new songs with simple words. The best dancers perform solo or in pairs in the centre. The chorus remains seated, moving and singing to the rhythm of the drums. When no special dance is under way, a

small boy may occupy the centre, dancing in kebyar style, controlling the chorus and calling 'Stop!' (in English) when the music comes to a good place to break off.

After dinner we heard the beating of a distant gong, growing louder as a procession of children and followers approached through the darkness. The twelve girls were already wearing their

A janger performance under way in the hotel garden . . .

. . . And here is a wider view of the same event, with audience.

homemade crowns, with their faces made up with yellow powder, eyebrows lined with burnt cork and lips smeared with red sireh juice. A stiffened lock of hair hung in front of each ear. The twelve boys wore dirty, ragged shorts, had faces smeared with chalk and sprouted moustaches under pug noses.

While they formed their square, Sabah set lamps at each corner and six musicians settled down under a tree with gongs, drums and cymbals. Renoh, a jongos, sat with them and played sad, rippling tunes on his flute. Leekas took over one of the drums, to lend a professional touch. The crowd from the villages gathered around, spellbound naked children in front.

The performance began with a miscarriage of rhythm and an answering ripple of titters from the audience. A little girl forgot her gestures and continually fell behind, earning pokes and severe glances from her neighbours. Two boys collided when they lost their timing. One with a perfect Hitler moustache pinched another and raised his arm in defence. Another left in the middle of a number to answer a call of nature. Yet the angular, feminine gestures and high, thin voices of the girls and the boys' rough motions and hoarse cries captured the feeling of even a polished janger.

Star of the show was a six-year-old soloist. Her round, fat face was a miniature of dignity though wisps of hair stuck out in disorder from her crown and her fat stomach burst out between her blouse and sarong. Her sarong slid slowly down until one of the musicians stepped in to hitch it up, like the invisible property man of the Chinese theatre.

She followed the rhythm on pudgy feet with plump toes turned out and short arms swaying. Her fingers moved a little only when she put her mind to it, but her head slid easily and her eyes flashed, shoulders shimmied and hips swayed.

The words accompanying the tunes were either a repetition of meaningless syllables or childish dialogue, such as:

Girls — We saw you coming to market this morning. What for?

Boys — To buy sugar and look at the girls.

Girls — We hope when you marry us you will have only one wife.

Boys — We'll not marry you.

Girls — We don't want you either. Go home and wash your faces. They are dirty.

All together — Ke-cak! Ke-cak! Ke-cak!

The untrained actors scrambled through to the grand finale produced by the six smallest boys. They pretended to go into a trance, shivering and jerking to indicate that spirits were entering their bodies. After attacking a lad dressed in a homemade Rangda costume, they turned their small krisses on themselves and flopped up and down on their backs, like stranded fish. We feared they would injure themselves but found that their krisses were of wood with blunt ends. Their performance was so realistic that we were startled when one dropped out of character with a smile. The whole trance act, right to realistic revivals, was a beautiful piece of mimicry.

This first performance, the best of the three, was so moving in its childish clumsiness that Donald and Zorka wanted to contribute towards better costumes. I suggested the best policy would be to give them two guilders at most and let them earn the rest. We paid them a few cents a performance, gradually increasing over several months to $2.50. Costumes and proficiency improved with each show but in a way nothing could equal that first one by inexpert little hoodlums.

Leekas, fearing that the children might lose their enthusiasm, always gave ten cents to the most lively performer and a penny each to others for not relaxing out of character. A regular winner, it turned out, was Dag, the boy who stopped the chorus to start each new number. Eventually Dag's picture would appear on the cover of Life magazine, with the girls in the background. His ability and charm were so great that we asked Mario to come from Tabanan to see him.

Mario grasped the boy's wrists from behind and danced measures of the kebyar, sweeping Dag along with him. As he released him for a moment, the serious-faced child went on as his imagination dictated until Mario doubled up in laughing delight. During an hour of teaching, the only changes in Dag's expression were those which accompanied the dance.

'Splendid! Number One!' said Mario when we asked his opinion. 'He will make a good kebyar dancer.'

We offered to pay for Dag's lessons, Mario wanted to teach him, the boy wanted to learn — but his conservative old father refused to let him go to Tabanan.

After the group had made enough for new costumes, further earnings went to parties for themselves or were divided evenly, regardless of ability, among all members. As in all Balinese amateur dancing and drama companies (the vast majority of them) the individual earned nothing. Earnings were communally owned and were spent according to majority vote.

But as soon as the routines became tedious and the novelty wore off, the club disbanded.

A month after the janger competition, we saw one of Bali's oldest dances, brought up to date with a big production chorus.

Two days earlier, the Bali Hotel had been awaiting seven important passengers on the noon plane. But the group, which included very senior people in Pan American Airways, the mayor of Los Angeles, the publisher of the Baltimore Sun and other dignitaries, drove to our hotel instead.

▲ *Dag, a talented discovery, entrances his audience with gesture, expression and charm. Mario wanted to teach him and we would have paid for his lessons, but his conservative father refused to let him go to Tabanan.*

One of the Pan American people, 'Sonny' Whitney, asked if we had room for them all.

'Of course,' Bob said, thinking fast. One would have to stay in a long abandoned 'temporary' cottage which now leant at a picturesque angle.

'I'll take it,' said Mr Whitney. 'It suits me perfectly.'

Then the Bali Hotel manager phoned with a message for the seven travellers. Their lunch was ready and waiting.

'But they're staying with us,' Bob said.

'I don't understand. There must be some mistake.'

'I don't think so. They intended to stay here.'

'Did they make reservations with you?'

'No, but they didn't make them with you either.'

'That wasn't necessary. Of course we expected them.'

'Awfully sorry,' Bob said. 'They've decided to stay here.'

We derived a mean satisfaction from this incident which can be fully appreciated only by someone who has attempted to compete (even on our miniscule scale) with a powerful near-monopoly.

The seven Americans were looking at business conditions in east Asia, but in Bali wanted to see outstanding entertainment. By unprecedented good luck, a village seventeen miles away was about to stage a traditional sanghyang dance, or trance dance, for the first time in years, and there would be two modern kecak performances as well. The villagers in the area had been suffering badly from malaria and were performing the sanghyang so a girl medium could ask help from the gods. Leekas went off to make arrangements.

On the evening of the performance, we were led to chairs on the edge of a large clearing. Hundreds of villagers from miles around milled about. There was a long wait — nothing to the Balinese but tiring to tense Europeans — before activity drew us to where a girl of about ten was bending over a dish of smoking coconut shells and incense. Two priestesses held her arms. After a few minutes the child began to sway, her eyes closed and her head wobbling.

The priestesses, working gently lest they waken her, dressed the girl in an elaborate costume. When she was ready, a man lifted her to one shoulder and carried her carefully to the platform. A chorus of fifty women sitting on the ground sang a sad minor tune. To left and right, the two kecaks, each of a hundred and fifty men wearing only loin cloths, sat in tight, concentric circles around a lamp-stand with seven coconut shells holding coconut oil. Burning wicks threw a soft light on the faces and bodies of the waiting dancers.

The girl danced with eyes closed, her raised arms and bent knees following the style of the legong. As the women stopped singing, one of the kecaks began chanting. Deep, full voices broke into what sounded like a college cheer. Bodies swayed in unison and three hundred arms rose, extended fingers trembling in the light of the oil lamps. The whole mass fell back with a shout, shoulders on the knees of those behind. Up again, arms and bodies weaving like young trees in the wind. A hissing and soughing of wind through the leaves, the croak of frogs and the angry hissing of excited monkeys.

A priest with hair to his waist delivered a long exhortation. As he withdrew, the chorus sang a melody which rose from a whisper to a roar. A lone figure dressed as a monkey rose from the mass, a red hibiscus over one ear. He pulled himself up until he seemed to be eight feet tall. He postured and pranced around the lamp stand.

A man joined him, and both melted back into the field of quivering, outstretched hands.

The girl continued dancing in time to the chanting.

As one kecak group ended, the other took over, following a similar pattern but telling a different story. At the climax two armies of monkeys did battle. Half the dancers rose to their feet, hissing in fury, arms and fingers reaching to catch the lamplight. As they fell back, the other half rose in a wrathful wave. Then both were up and at each other in stylised combat.

The women resumed singing and the girl, with a flower and a jar of holy water, sprinkled the heads and extended hands of people crowding near, seeking a blessing. She opened her eyes, was led away, her dancer's helmet was removed, and very soon she was a little village girl once more.

As the war drew nearer and tourists became fewer, dance companies had to try harder to attract audiences. The village of Bona let it be known it was going to perform an improper dance. I asked some of our guests if they would like to see something said to be 'quite shocking'. They were conservative people, so I was surprised when they said yes.

So one night we came to be seated before a great temple gateway while the village headman whispered to me that what we were going to see was so special that we should engage it often. The whole village of Bona had gathered and there was an unusual amount of chatter and rude laughter. Light came from a lamp with seven coconut shells, like the one used in the kecak.

The gay and stimulating music of the flirtation dance rang out, and a matron of about thirty — instead of a girl in traditional costume — stepped out. She was plump, with heavy breasts scarcely anchored by her lowcut blouse. She wore a cap of flowers, black seeds the size of pigeon's eggs distended her pierced earlobes, and her sarong was black.

After dancing alone, she was joined by a lanky, horse-faced man who parodied her every move. He waved his buttocks and, standing still, pushed down his sarong and rolled the muscles of his belly. He sucked in his stomach until it seemed to touch his spine, then pushed it out as if he had a large tumor. The crowd roared with laughter.

The woman's strong and limber body became serpentine and suggestive. Crude invitation travelled from her drooping eyelids to her writhing hips. A tall, slender man leapt towards her, pushing the clown off the floor. He crouched, his face eager with passion, his fingers reaching for her, his hard muscles taut. Man and woman watched each other like duellists. The man crouched still lower, hopping, advancing, retreating. Leaping, he circled the woman's shoulders with one arm, not touching her but sniffing at her neck. His pelvis jerked. The crowd yelled.

The headman whispered, 'Is it all right to make it funny? If you wish, I'll stop it.'

'It's all right,' I said.

A priest with hair falling down his back came striding in, and delivered a tirade against the libidinous pair. They bowed their heads in shame. The priest withdrew. The pair sneaked back to the centre of the floor and threw themselves into a pattern of sexual spasms. The woman rolled her hips and the man threw his pelvis forward in sharp, strong thrusts. Whenever he seemed to lag, the women moved to the lamp stand and, her face fully lit, looked to some place offstage, her eyebrows raised, her lips pursed.

I looked apprehensively at our guests. The only disapproval I saw came not from them but from Bob — he was worried about our hotel's reputation.

The dancers were shining with sweat. The man manoeuvred to get behind the woman and gestured as if to leap on her back. She slid smoothly to one side. When it seemed that at any minute nothing would be left to the imagination, a third man, lean and muscular like the first, ran in, flourishing two swords. The two men danced a stylised fight with open hands, then picked up the swords and continued, lunging and parrying.

There was no evidence of victory but the first dancer seemed to be the winner. The other walked casually away. The winner rushed headlong to the woman, swept her up in his arms and carried her towards the rendezvous she had been suggesting with her eyes.

Our guests were delighted but Bob was worried.

'We can't risk it again,' he said.

But we did. I continued to take selected tourists — while Bob stayed home.

War clouds blow nearer

Our fourth Christmas in Bali was ushered in by the arrival of a two-seater aircraft which landed on the beach in front of the hotel. Two British pilots from Singapore climbed out and asked for rooms.

'Our little crate will be all right hitched to your fence,' one said, 'if we can get her over the soft sand.'

'Hold everything,' said Bob. 'I'll get some boards and the boys will help push her up.'

While boards were being found and the pushing began, I asked one of the pilots if the plane were their own.

'Yes, it's our vacation bus,' he said. 'We hop around in it when we get a few days off. Nice, isn't it?' He patted a blue wing affectionately.

That night, with the plane tethered to our fence, the boys put on a super-parade to announce dinner, spending twice the usual amount on firecrackers. The next day, they were taken up one by one on short flights, returning with stars in their eyes and laughing exultantly. After a week the plane looked quite at home in our front yard, though its informal hops into the sky still brought all the servants running.

Preparations for Christmas went all-out. I made stockings of mosquito netting, filled them with small gifts and hung them outside each cottage door, early, before anyone was up. An evergreen tree from the mountains filled one corner of the dining room,

glistening with decorations from the Japanese Household Goods Emporium. The boys put little presents for us underneath and festooned the whole room with coconut fronds until it looked like an American version of a tropical night club.

Outside the door, looking out to sea, two sentinal bamboos rose twenty feet and drooped at their tips with the weight of bell-shaped straw decorations and bouquets of laden rice stems. Such decorated bamboos when used during a particular Balinese festival turned the roads and lanes into lacy arcades. Now we had two of our own.

'What does Christmas mean?' Leekas asked.

'It is the day Christ was born, 1939 years ago.'

'Who was Christ?'

'He was the son of our god. Some Christians make offerings to him and his mother.'

'Then your religion is like ours. We have one god but he has many faces.'

'How can you believe in one god when you have so many? Each village has several.'

'The high priests know there is only one, but the people cannot understand. They call him by different names. Still, we have only one so he must be the same as yours.'

'How about Rangda? You make offerings to her. Is she not a god too — an evil one?'

'Have you nothing like Rangda?'

'We have, only it's male, the devil. But we have no leyaks.'

'You have no leyaks?'

'Well, yes, we call them ghosts.'

'What is "ghost"?'

'Ghosts are people who have died. They look like smoke. You can see through them. They walk at night to frighten the living.'

'Then our god is the same,' Leekas concluded, 'only we have different customs.'

Indeed we have different customs, but with war threatening to engulf the world I could not recommend ours to a Balinese.

◄ *Decorated bamboo poles turn a village street into a lacy arcade.*
— a spectacle repeated throughout the island.

At lunch on May 10, 1940, we talked about the possibility of Holland being invaded. A German guest, a planter from Java, was the only one who ridiculed the idea. Hitler had promised to respect Holland's neutrality, he said, and we were letting rumours play on our minds.

In the middle of the afternoon, the Controleur arrived from Denpasar with four policemen. Holland had been invaded. All our Dutch friends had families in their home country, in some cases wives and children. To us the news meant — had we faced it — the beginning of the end.

The Controleur asked for our German guest. He was on the beach. We sent a jongos.

'We'll wait,' said the Controleur. 'He's the last.'

All Germans in Bali were being arrested, including Walter Spies, so recently released from his time in prison for being a homosexual. He and many other people died when two ships taking prisoners to Ceylon (now Sri Lanka) were sunk by the Japanese off the coast of Sumatra.

A few minutes later, the German ran in from the beach in his bathing suit, in a hurry to get his camera to photograph a procession. He saw the Controleur and the policemen, and understood. He smiled sorrowfully as the Controleur said he could take his time dressing.

He came to the dining room for afternoon tea. The policemen watched through the open door. Bob asked him what he thought of Hitler's guarantees.

'I can't understand it,' he muttered, holding his cup with two hands to stop the trembling. 'Everything's gone. My plantation — my work of thirteen years — everything I have in the world.'

He was so crushed that we believed he was not one of Hitler's agents, as so many other Germans were, with Hitler's photograph

⋏ Another woman poses, arranging flowers in her hair.

264

on their walls and with congratulations on their birthdays over the German radio. That same day the Dutch foiled a German plot to take over Surabaya, mainly because a girl in the telegraph office wondered why so many important Germans in the town were receiving identical coded messages. She sensed something was wrong and told the police.

Two days later I took a telephone call from the new manager of the Bali Hotel, and was lectured severely when I answered in English. Since I did not speak Dutch, I must speak in Malay, I was told, because all conversations were censored and languages other than Dutch and Malay were not to be used.

This was a switch. Not long before I had spoken Malay to a party of Dutch people from Java because they could not speak English. Immediately they turned their backs and walked disdainfully away. It seemed no Dutch person ever spoke Malay to a social equal — I had been treating them like servants.

All able-bodied Dutch men in the Indies were called in for military training. Native volunteers squeezed their splayed feet into heavy boots and their bodies into khaki uniforms. Bombers spent two days a week at the Bali airport just along the beach from our hotel while their crews got target practice.

Before long Bob would find himself tearing up his five-hole golf course at the airport. A bulldozer had been sent to do the job but its Balinese driver had no idea what was needed. So Bob took pleasure running the machine himself, obeying orders by tearing great holes in the ground but also piling up earth to elaborate the hazards and form bunkers for the four unfinished holes. Every day he returned tired and dusty, but pleased. He was an optimist virtually to the end.

The home guard swarmed over the beach and through the coconut trees at Sanur, practising machine-gunning. A large part of the local population immediately fled inland to live with friends and relatives. Then it was our turn. At 2 a.m. we heard the rattle of machine-gun fire.

'Now they're practising here,' Bob said. 'Poor devils. It's raining and black as pitch.'

The next morning, two hundred villagers left Kuta. The Chinese shopkeepers were building or renting houses in the mountains, and their wives and children filtered away as well. Our boys found

reason also to send their wives and children to other parts of Bali.

A few guests still lingered with us in 1941, mostly businessmen from other parts of the Indies. Tourists from Australia and Singapore were first discouraged and then stopped by the difficulty of getting money out of their countries. A few American airmen visited us, some from teaching in Java, some on their way to join General Chenault's Flying Tigers in China.

A Japanese mission to Batavia to seek special trade concessions had failed. The Japanese radio blamed Dutch stubbornness and said that 'stronger steps' would follow. If this meant steps towards Java, they would have first to capture the airfield on Bali, so defences were built.

Powerful lights and machine-guns were installed and several hundred village men were engaged to come from miles around at a moment's notice to dig obstructions. At a dress rehearsal, they showed up frightened and disorganised, accompanied by families and friends bearing camping equipment, rice, chickens and pigs. The army had second thoughts and decided on removable hurdles of heavy timber instead.

A tank trap several hundred yards long was dug across the road to the airport. Men and women toiled for days, digging, lining the ditch with tarred teak logs, camouflaging the result with small trees. Hundreds of coconut trees were felled and many huts moved inland on rollers to make room for a new road along the beach from our hotel to the airport.

I asked a fisherman what he thought the road was for. 'So people can run away faster when the enemy comes,' he said.

Balinese soldiers dug holes in the sand and planted long coconut logs along the beach. Miles of them bristled all the way from the airport to beyond our hotel. Each tide washed a few away and undermined others, leaving them at crazy angles. Patient, khaki-clad men came out to rebuild their battle stage.

A barbed wire fence, three rows deep, was built along our beach and at Sanur, wherever roads led directly to Denpasar. Our

◄ Bob with one of the sand 'greens' of the miniature golf course he built around the hotel. He had begun work on a larger one near the airport when the war ruined everything.

Dutch friends still came down every Sunday to swim, but now they had to make their way to the sea through a series of irregular openings, holding their clothes away from the barbs and balancing surfboards overhead.

Our boys continually asked for news. We showed them maps and explained that the war might come to Bali.

'See this point?' I said. 'This very, very little dot that you can

▲ Our hotel from the sea, before we built the beach pergola. The large building is the dining room.

hardly find? Well, that's Bali.'

'How is it possible?' they laughed. 'And look at Java — how small it is too.'

In spite of the spreading alarm, Bob never lost his belief in a miracle — right up to Pearl Harbour. Long after Holland was invaded, he built an elaborate pergola by the sand. As the hotel by this time was no more than paying its way, I thought the expense unwarranted, but our enterprise had succeeded through taking chances and Bob could not admit we might be facing defeat.

The pergola provided shade and a view of the sea through vine-covered pillars. Two old outrigger canoes dripping with morning glories were mounted on each side. There was a two-foot wall along the front for potted plants and for sitting or spreading wet towels. And there was a barbecue pit where we had informal outdoor lunches with Rankop and Tampa broiling weenies and pork sate. It was an elegant addition to the hotel, and a shame we did not have tourists to enjoy it.

As if the pergola were not enough, in the second half of 1941 Bob talked himself into expecting a Christmas rush from Java, and

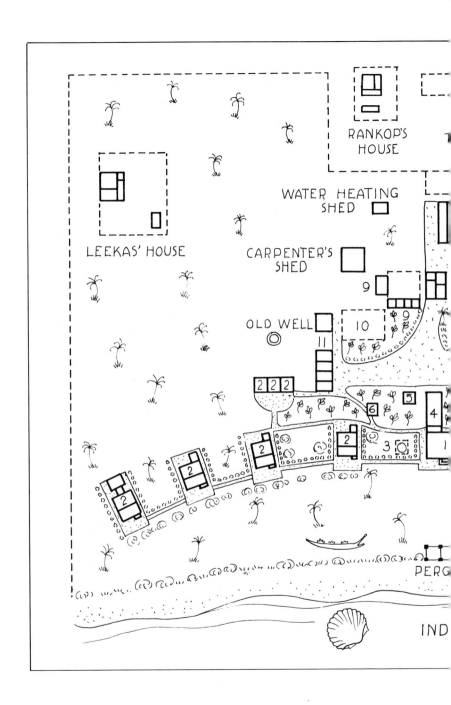

RANKOP'S
HOUSE

WATER HEATING
SHED

LEEKAS' HOUSE

CARPENTER'S
SHED

9

OLD WELL

10

9

11

2 2 2

6

5

4

2

2

2

3

1

PERG

IND

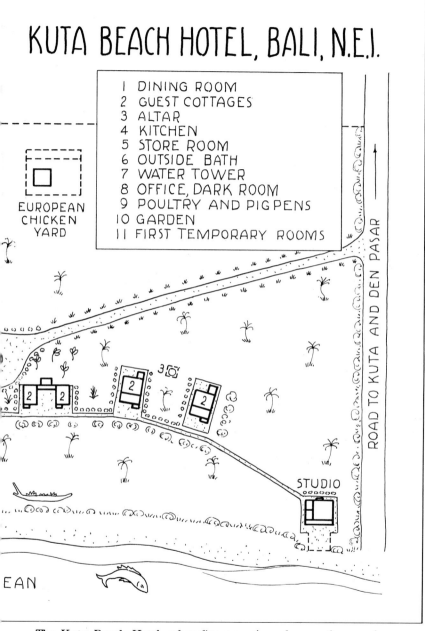

KUTA BEACH HOTEL, BALI, N.E.I.

1 DINING ROOM
2 GUEST COTTAGES
3 ALTAR
4 KITCHEN
5 STORE ROOM
6 OUTSIDE BATH
7 WATER TOWER
8 OFFICE, DARK ROOM
9 POULTRY AND PIG PENS
10 GARDEN
11 FIRST TEMPORARY ROOMS

EUROPEAN CHICKEN YARD

ROAD TO KUTA AND DEN PASAR

STUDIO

EAN

The Kuta Beach Hotel, after five years' work — a far cry from our modest ideas in 1936.

built three extra bedrooms under one roof. While he landscaped the new building's front yard, I hurried the furniture makers and ordered more stone dragons to match those guarding the steps of all the other cottages. The rooms were ready early in December.

Early in the morning of the sixth day of that month (the seventh on the other side of the world), Bob was listening to the radio.

'It's another one of those Orson Welles stories about the future,' he said. 'Now he's got Pearl Harbour being bombed.'

A few minutes later — 'My God! It's real! It's actually happening. I'll go for the guests.' He bolted out the door in his pyjamas.

Our eight guests, all Dutch, one still wet from a dawn swim, the others in their night clothes and wrappers, pressed around the radio, the men spluttering with profanities, the women speechless. Within two hours the hotel was empty, each man leaving for his appointed station in the defence of Java.

A blackout was declared. We shrouded our lamps with improvised covers and stopped dining on the lawn. Driving a car at night became almost impossible as we were allowed only a narrow slit in each headlight. Denpasar died after dark. All over the island, the Balinese were forbidden to use their kerosene lamps out of doors, so night entertainment ceased. Not even a roadside stall cheered people walking home late.

By day, people huddled in worried knots, talking about a war so distant that it had not even touched Java but which in some unaccountable way menaced Bali. For the first time people in remote villages learned there was a war and that they might become involved. Air raid shelters grew like giant molehills in the yards of Denpasar homes. Our boys began digging trenches in our grounds. They were fearful of bombs, imagining one would wipe out a whole village (which struck me as amusing in that pre-atomic era).

They knew nothing about the Japanese as the few families on the island had kept to themselves, but disliked them on principle because of their sympathy for the Chinese in the war in China. To try to allay anxiety, we explained that the Japanese were not angry with them and that their objective was to rid East Asia of white people and take over.

We tried to find out what they felt about a Japanese occupation. None of them could imagine a life other than the one they knew under the generally fair and civilised Dutch. The only other kind of rule they had heard of was that of the rajas before the Dutch took over — and that was too unreal to happen again. Old people's stories about how autocratic rajas sacrificed their subjects in wars between each other were more like legends, now that life was pleasant and secure. And as for the rajas who thought nothing of cutting out tongues, gouging out eyes or lopping off hands for slight or imagined offences — that sort of thing was just hard to believe.

Mario came to visit, sitting dejectedly on the floor. For the first time he did not smile. He remembered vaguely about the Dutch attack on Denpasar when he was a small boy. The royal family and their retainers had marched out of the palace armed with krisses to meet certain death from foreign rifles. They forced the Dutch to mow them down and those who remained killed each other and themselves.

This war would be even more horrifying, because he had seen photographs in our magazines of aircraft dropping bombs.

It had taken him and most other Balinese a long time to realise that the future looked black. But then, we were just as blind, and we should have known better. A week passed after Pearl Harbour before we began to come to our senses.

'Don't you think it's time to go?' I asked Bob. He had just phoned American consulates in Java to ask if there was anything he could do. The consulates said they had no need of him and advised us to return home.

'Since they have all the help they want, what's the point of waiting here?' I continued. 'Do you want to die in a Japanese concentration camp?'

'Concentration camp?' Bob exclaimed in surprise. 'I don't think the Japanese will ever get here, but still I should get into the American army in Java. I'll have to go to headquarters to apply. They're a small unit but they might be able to use me as an interpreter, or I could help in construction work.'

We agreed to take what we could in the car and drive to Surabaya. If Bob succeeded in getting into the army, I would return home alone — not to avoid being imprisoned by the Japanese but for a much needed change of climate. That was a reason Bob could admit to.

*Bali in 1941, despite talk of war, was relaxed, continuing its
rounds of festivals and ceremonies in timeless manner. But the
Japanese were drawing nearer.*

Departure

Paralyzed by the idea of leaving Bob for a year or two, perhaps for ever, I wandered aimlessly for two days. Bob wandered with me, and then precipitated action by setting December 31 for our departure. We made it final by telling our friends. Anxiety about the fate of families in Holland, already long in German hands, and the shadow of approaching disaster in the Indies was suppressed in friendly trivialities. We visited people in their darkened homes and joked with them about what we should bring back for them. Officials' wives were still with them because the government had ordered that the Balinese were not to be alarmed, even by the departure of women.

Leekas agreed to be responsible for the hotel, so long as he had a letter from the Controleur saying he was our agent. Bob warned that there might be no more guests and said he would leave enough money for Leekas and two or three men for a year.

'You will have to make all the decisions yourself,' Bob continued. 'If you have trouble, go to the Controleur or the Assistant Controleur, or the bank manager. They want to help.'

I stocked the store room well with canned goods, kerosene and two hundred pounds of rice. Bob bought more cases of liquor and soft drinks and paid the telephone bill for January.

'The turkeys and chickens will feed you well,' he told Leekas. 'If the Japanese come, take as many as you can for yourself.'

Our several hundred books and Bob's darkroom equipment had

to be left behind. I rolled my paintings in a tarpaulin. We examined the few warm garments we had brought with us and aired once a week through the years. We drew our remaining money out of the bank. After we had sold the car and bought passage home to America we would have about $1000 — just the amount we had gone into business with five years before. All the rest of the money we had made had gone back into improving the hotel, which the books showed to have cost more than $10,000.

I overheard Bob remonstrating with the famous concert pianist, Lili Kraus*, who was determined to go on tour in Sumatra.

'You're out of your mind,' Bob said. 'You can't do it.'

Pretty good for Bob, I thought, who habitually denied that there was any danger. He was coming out of his trance.

The boys still did not understand why we must go. With the Japanese making steady gains towards Singapore, we tried to give them some idea of what was happening outside their island. When Bob tried to explain that in order to fight he had to go to the United States, they shrugged. If the fighting was to be in Bali, why not stay and fight in Bali?

Their reasoning was simple and direct in all matters. With a map, we spent an hour telling Leekas about Hitler's rapidly rising fortunes and about the Japanese onslaught. We thought 'we got across a rather good description of the attack on Pearl Harbour, and worked up to the idea that the Japanese were now uncomfortably close to Bali. We tried to tell him what we thought life would be like under the Japanese. Then we asked him to tell us what he thought would happen if Bali were taken.

He looked towards the Dutch flag flying from a bamboo pole on the beach nearby. 'We must change the flag to the sign of the red ball,' he said.

*It seems Lili Kraus did go on tour, despite Bob's advice. At least, she and her husband did not leave the Indies — the Japanese captured them in Batavia (now Jakarta) and they spent the war years in a prison camp. After the war she regained her stature as an outstanding musician. Lili Kraus died in North Carolina in 1986, aged 81.

'Why must you go?' le Meyeur asked as we sat drinking wine in his arbor. Polok, his beautiful wife, was beside him, her light brown skin as smooth as satin. 'Nothing's going to happen here.'

'Don't you realise that Bali must fall before Java?'

Le Meyeur looked at us as if we were either lunatics or pathologically stupid.

'This is the time to think fast,' Bob said.

Le Meyeur remained in his world of fantasy. Polok in the flower-strewn fields of his paintings was real. The rest was hysteria.

'I'm going to stay right here and nothing is going to happen to me,' he said, 'although I may send Polok to the mountains where she'll feel safer. But let's not worry any more about this. Have dinner with me on Christmas Day. And tell Leekas to come to me if anything goes wrong at the hotel. I'll be glad to help him.'

We spent the last evening with government officials and their wives. Twelve of us had dinner at a Chinese restaurant. The men were calm and reserved. I looked at their pretty, delicate young wives and wondered if they and their golden-haired children would survive if the worst happened. Some were run down from malaria and all needed a rest from the tropics. Their children were already a transparent white. All home leave had been cancelled since the fall of Holland. They were so gallant, these trapped people, as we pretended it was just like any other night in the happy past.

'Tell Leekas he can count on us if he needs help,' they said as we shook hands and wished each other luck.

The next morning we stood awkwardly by the car in the first light of dawn. The coconut trees were ghostly in the dripping mist. Our ten remaining servants stood in a semi-circle around us and made stammering, formal speeches of farewell. They wished us luck, asked us to write, hoped we would return after the war.

'You can write to me in English,' Leekas said proudly.

Tears choked us. We were leaving our home. We were leaving the life we had built up over five years. Bob stalled by delivering yet another lecture on what should be done if the Japanese came.

I wanted to hug these small people with their sad faces and gay sarongs, although such is not the custom in Bali and might cause embarrassment. At the last minute I put an arm around Leekas' bare shoulder and pressed my cheek to his for an instant.

The Chevrolet was packed. We got in and Bob fumbled blindly for the starter. As he drove down the coral drive, he sobbed and tears ran down his pale cheeks.

As we turned through the gate to the road, I looked back at the brown, thatched cottages dotted through the coconut grove, at the great water tower, at the yards where our fat turkeys and chickens still slept.

'Leekas will run the hotel almost as well as we could,' I said. 'He might have a few people from Java now and then, and you know how conscientious he is. He will send you the most careful accounting. He will watch for termites and see that the mattresses don't get mouldy.'

But I was thinking about the machine-gun emplacements in the grounds, and the barbed wire fences, and the airfield almost next door. It would take little to reduce the buildings to rubble and the grove to a field of stumps.

'We have to go through Tabanan,' Bob said. 'Shall we stop to say goodbye to Mario?'

'No. He wouldn't understand. It would take a long explanation,' I said.

But my real reason was that I did not want to see him for the last time. I wanted to remember him with eyes twinkling and one eyebrow playfully raised.

Surabaya had become a different city. Long lines of earth-coloured army trucks moved slowly along the main boulevard, full of small Javanese soldiers or tall Americans. Jeeps and armoured cars bristling with machine-guns slowed the traffic. The sidewalks were crowded with Dutch, American and Australian sailors. American dollars flooded the shops and hotels. Shop windows were latticed with paper and cloth strips to reduce flying glass from bomb explosions. Before dawn almost every morning we heard Flying Fortress and Liberator bombers setting out on missions from Malang.

The Dutch went about business and pleasure as usual. The clubs were filled to capacity every afternoon and evening. One night the Oranje Hotel supplied dinner for three busloads of young men and women in full evening dress. A Dutch friend was obliged to take two days out of his fevered schedule to act as proxy at an ultra-formal dinner.

Bob wooed American army officers but they could only advise him to return home for training. Daily we trudged from one shipping company to another, reminding them that we were still waiting. The last passenger ship for the United States had left soon after Pearl Harbour but freighters were still taking their chances of getting through the constantly tightening blockade of enemy submarines.

We gathered every bit of news we could to learn what ships were sailing. As idle waiting got on our nerves, the idea of getting back home became an obsession. So many reports filtered through of ships sunk in nearby waters that we feared we might not leave at all.

A letter arrived from Leekas.

'We having three guests from Australia in Number One and Two. I charge less because hotel are empty. They say they like here. Tampa is cooking. Sabah is jongos. Tuan Controleur comes often. He says he will help if I am needing him. He says I keep hotel very clean. . . . You shall not worry. I will take care of everything.'

A month after we arrived in Surabaya, I was sitting in the clubhouse at the golf club while Bob was playing. A caddy ran up and said Bob wanted me at once. I found him with his Javanese companion and three more caddies on top of a long hill. All were scanning the intensely blue sky. The city lay beneath us with the port beyond.

One of the caddies shouted, 'Look! Over there!'

We saw a tiny speck in the sky, then more, and the sound of engines and the rat-tat-tat of machine-gun fire. One dot chased another in a long, swift curve. Fighters were dog-fighting.

The bombers followed, with deeper-sounding engines, in threes — twentysix of them.

'Chop bola,' the Javanese golfer said, referring to the round ball sign we could see on the aircraft, the sign of Japan. As they flew past they seemed like glass toys, shining perhaps with light reflected from the sea. It was too beautiful and shocking a sight for us to realise fully what was happening. Anti-aircraft shells popped under the planes' bellies, blossoming into bouquets of smoke. The planes held formation and turned across the city. We heard explosions and huge clouds of smoke rose here and there in the far distance.

Back in the city, down the main shopping street, we saw no serious damage but windows were shattered and glass littered the sidewalks. Up the side streets were craters twelve feet across. A strong wind had blown the bombs slightly to one side, sparing the important buildings and making a shambles of the native quarter behind. Silent Javanese pulled and poked at the wreckage of their homes and bullock carts were carrying away the bodies. The building next to our second-class hotel was in ruins.

On February 4 we arrived in the primitive port town of Tjilatjap (now spelt Cilacap) on the south coast of Java. As it was considered the least dangerous port, all shipping was being sent here. We had accommodation on a Dutch ship, the Poelau Roebiah. Other passengers arrived, oil men from Borneo and Sumatra and missionaries with their children from distant islands who had reached Java in small sailing praus. The ship was loading hemp, tea, chrome, sago and rubber.

The following day, the 10,000-ton cruiser USS Houston steamed in slowly, her rear turret charred and gutted from action in the Java Sea. She had come in to unload dead and wounded before returning to the fight, and to her end in the Sunda Straits. The slightly smaller USS Marblehead came in with more dead and wounded, so badly damaged she could not fight any more. Eventually she reached home. That night we heard carpenters hammering, making fifty coffins.

When we sailed our captain told us to keep our life jackets with us at all times and to remain fully dressed at night. 'I have to tell you that there are many enemy submarines,' he said. 'Many ships have been sunk near here.' We were at sea for fortytwo zigzagging days before arriving in New York.

Long before we got there Bali had fallen to the Japanese. We told each other we hoped the boys were safe, but there was no way of finding out.

Return to Bali

It was still practically dark, one morning in March, 1946, when Bob climbed into the Douglas C-47 in Surabaya. In less than two hours — after exactly four years, three months and six days away — he would be 'home' again, back in Bali, while I was still far away in the United States. Although it was a full six months since the Japanese surrender, the Dutch landing and occupation of the island was just two days under way.

In Bali, on the clear, wide beach at Kuta, we had built our particular castle in the air, a very special kind of hotel with separate bungalows under coconut trees. For five happy years we played host to Americans, Dutch, British, French, Swiss, South Africans, Australians . . . we began to think of Bali as the true crossroads of the world. Actually, the Balinese do think it so, and not just a pinpoint on the globe.

For almost four years virtually no news had come out of the island. For most of this time Bob was in the American Army with the South-East Asia Command. Reports had come through, after the Japanese surrender, that our hotel, like all other houses abandoned by the Europeans, had been looted and its building materials carried away. From his army experience, Bob well understood looting and was not hurt by this news that the Balinese had scavenged what the Japanese had left. What really mattered was what had happened to the Balinese, to our old friends Leekas, Rankop, Tampa, Mario and others who were still more real to him than army routine.

The aircraft passed the eastern tip of Java and headed along Bali's south coast. Wind and rain forced it down to one hundred feet. The pilot had almost decided to return to Surabaya when the weather broke and Bob glimpsed a road running down to the sea. It looked like the road which had run beside our hotel, but the site seemed bare. They flew on the couple of miles to the airstrip, 'buzzed' it to clear away wandering cows and landed on the grass runway.

A truck was about to leave for Denpasar, Bob got a lift, and was soon in the Bali Hotel, now the Dutch military headquarters. He looked up two correspondent friends from Batavia, and they told him they were going to Sanur to have lunch with le Meyeur and his wife. Bob did not think le Meyeur and Polok would mind if he went along too.

While they were waiting for a car, Bob saw a Balinese man we had known well over several years. He was elated to see Bob — at first. Then his expression changed to one of uneasy aloofness. Perhaps it was his formal, normal manners returning. The car arrived, they said goodbye and Bob put the unpleasant impression out of his mind.

Le Meyeur and Polok were startled and pleased when Bob arrived so unexpectedly. Le Meyeur had not been interned and they had lived through the occupation with a certain degree of comfort. Though his house had been looted by the Balinese at Japanese orders, le Meyeur had been able to keep most of his paintings. His latest ones were on burlap for lack of canvas and suggested old tapestries. He had enough pictures for another exhibition in Singapore.

It was a pleasant lunch and Polok did a dance for them afterwards. But le Meyeur took Bob aside to tell him that no Balinese would dare be seen talking to a white man, especially one in an American army uniform. Perhaps that had been the trouble with the man in Denpasar.

The next morning Bob was having breakfast when Made, our old laundryman, the best in the Far East, walked past with a pile of clean suits. Bob hurried after him and tapped him on the shoulder. Made dropped the suits and stood gulping, quite speechless. When words came, all he could say was, 'Are you all right?' over and over. Bob grasped his hand and felt his throat tighten as he saw how unchanged Made was.

Eventually he was able to tell Bob that he was head laundry-man at the Bali Hotel. He asked if we would build another hotel. Bob said he would have to go back to America first to get out of the army, but hoped to return, and that if he did Made could work for him again.

'Of course, Tuan,' he said. 'That is what I'm waiting for.'

But then he looked uneasy, perhaps nervous about being seen talking to a white man, glanced away, shuffled his feet and left. Later Bob sought him out in his laundry, where he presided over a force of women busy over tubs and ironing boards. Bob gave him some money and two bicycle tyres and tubes. He muttered his thanks and looked away, as if fearing someone had seen the transaction.

Thinking about the six months which had passed since the Japanese surrender gave Bob a sort of an answer. For six weeks no white men appeared. The Japanese remained in full control and the Balinese may have decided that the reported surrender was only a rumour.

Then two American planes landed with newspapermen who had seen the surrender ceremony in Japan, on their way to Australia. Doubtless this visit caused the grapevine to hum. But after two days the planes took off, and not a man stayed behind. What sort of victors were these? Two more months went by and the Balinese were more perplexed than ever.

Meanwhile, Indonesian Nationalists resisting the Dutch return to Java had come to Bali, and Indonesian flags appeared in Denpasar and Singaraja. Here was another angle for the Balinese to conjure with. A small Dutch ship came to Buleleng and thirty or forty Dutch men came ashore. They tore down an Indonesian flag, there was some fighting, and they left after a few hours. Balinese bewilderment increased.

Next came a small British group which received information and transport assistance from the Japanese, but stayed only four or five days. With the Japanese, Dutch, Americans, British and the Nationalists, the Balinese had ample cause to be confused. The Japanese had taught them for years that the white man had been exorcised for ever, and now the white men were behaving as if it were true. It was no wonder that a Balinese would not dare be seen talking to one of them.

*The war is over, the Japanese have gone — and so has the Kuta
Beach Hotel. This is all that Bob could find: An empty site, with
vague outlines of foundations and borders of daffodils growing
wild. It was almost as if the hotel had never existed.*

Bob learned that Tampa was living in Denpasar. His face lit up with a wide grin when Bob walked into his compound. 'Welcome, welcome,' he said. Bob wanted to ask him right away what the problem was with other people but that would not have been good manners. Instead they talked of Tampa's new wife and how happy he was with her. She had been his friend's wife, and his friend had liked Tampa's wife, so they had swapped and everyone was happy. He was planning to move back to his home town, Bangli, where he could not then be accused of collaborating with the Dutch, the Nationalists or anyone else.

He asked Bob if the Dutch were back to stay. What was the meaning of the three brief visits, and the delay? Bob answered as best he could but he could see that Tampa did not understand. It was disheartening to tell him that even his visit would be a short one. That put Bob in the same category as all the other white men who had been flying in and out.

Eventually Bob found his way to the site where our hotel once stood. The waves, the surf, the beach were unchanged but where the bungalows had been there was nothing. Nothing at all.

Even the coconut trees had been levelled. The only traces Bob could see, as he walked over the ground, were the vague outlines of the foundations and borders of daffodils growing wild. Even the bricks which lined the sumps beneath each bathroom had been scavenged, because bricks were worth one or two cents each.

A few people from Kuta village approached, timid but curious. Bob demonstrated by laughs and grins that he regarded the vanished buildings as a hilarious joke, and eventually was able to get them to talk to him. He pieced together what had happened.

The first Japanese assault troops had taken everything they could use — refrigerators, furniture, mattresses, china, cutlery. Then they told the Balinese that the white owners had been robbing them, and that everything remaining was theirs. Thatching and bamboo from the roofs, matting from the walls, wood from the frames, tiles from the floors — everything disappeared. They dug up the underground piping, which the Japanese had overlooked, but the military took it back from them. In Kuta village Bob saw a piece of panelling from our hotel built into the side of a house. The men he was with noticed that he recognised it, and he saved the situation by making it just another joke.

The coconut trees were felled when the occupation troops who followed the assault troops fortified the beach. The tree trunks went into machine-gun pits and other defences. It would be twenty years before the site could become a shady grove once more.

Bob met a man, Gati, who had been a chauffeur at the hotel. He made no bones about being friendly, pouring out a torrent of words. He had lost his old Buick to the Japanese but now had a fleet of dogcarts acquired mainly by barter with the Japanese.

'Why are your people so afraid?' Bob asked.

'There are rumours,' he said. 'They say the Nationalists from Java kill Balinese who associate with white people. And who knows if the Dutch will stay?'

Bob said they would, but Gati asked why they had not come for six months, and why small parties of white men came four times and left after only a few days.

Though he had his business, he was dressed in rags, like everyone else, because no cloth had been imported into Bali since before Pearl Harbour, more than four years before. Bob said that if he came to the corner near the Bali Hotel he would give him a new sarong. He itched to have it, but did not come.

Bob was unable to find Leekas. As he must have heard of his return, his failure to appear was a bitter blow, until Bob learned, much later, that Leekas had joined the Nationalist movement. He was intelligent enough to understand politics and courageous enough to risk his life for an ideal.

Mrs Katharane Mershon, one of the first people we met in Bali, later found Leekas in jail, a political prisoner. He had grown a long beard and was entirely occupied with religious studies. When he was released, he shaved off his beard and returned to what he had been doing before we met him, training a dance and drama company. This was what he had always liked best, and it is what Bali does best.

In the years which followed, as Bob and I pursued a completely different livelihood in different parts of the world, we naturally thought often about returning to Bali. But then, the five years we had there were a whole lifetime of satisfaction. It would have been tempting fate to try again. Bob has been back several times as a visitor but I prefer to remember Bali as it was.